COURTHOUSE PAINTING, JEFF PITTMAN

Call Your Next Case: My Stories

Copyright © 2024 by Judge "Rusty" Duke

All rights reserved. Except for brief excerpts for review purposes, no part of this book may be reproduced or used in any form without written permission from the author.

ISBN: 979-8-9918613-1-1

Editor, Bethany Bradsher

Cover design and interior layout by Stephanie Whitlock Dicken.

Courthouse Painting, Jeff Pittman. JeffPittmanArt@gmail.com

Pitt County Bar photograph, ASAP Photo and Video

All rights reserved worldwide.

CALL YOUR
NEXT CASE

CALL YOUR NEXT CASE

MY STORIES

JUDGE RUSTY DUKE

FOREWORD BY
RETIRED N.C. CHIEF JUSTICE MARK MARTIN

CHOCOWINITY PRESS

For the Jurors

Contents

For the Jurors 9
Dedication 13
Foreword 15

PART I: APPROACHING THE BENCH 19
An Overview of a Life in Court 21
The Judge's Call 25
The Big Democrat and the Dog 27
Electing Judges and the Bicycle Thief 29
The Most Enjoyable Job 33
The Days in the Life of a Superior Court Judge 36
Advice to a Young Judge 42
The Ruling is Final 45

PART II: TAKING CARE OF BUSINESS 47
Order in the Court 48
Control of the Courtroom 54
Lawyer Tough and Breakfast at McDonald's 56
Attention to the Court 62
Completing The Docket 64
We'll Pick a Jury at Two o'clock 69
TV and the Courtroom 75
The Courthouse 80

PART III: THE COURTROOM CREW 83
The Courthouse Redeemed 84
The Wonderful Jury 91
My Bailiffs 100
Experts 105
Working with Lawyers 109
Prosecutors 121
The Expectation of Professionalism 125
Whatcha Gonna Do? 130

PART IV: TALES FROM THE COURTROOM 133
A Judge 134
Parading Without a Permit 138
What's the Truth? 142
Peeling Potatoes 145
Out With the Old and In with the New 147
The Orphanage Offense 151
Plead Guilty 158
Lawrence, The Jury Foreman 161
Prayer Works... 164
The Criminal's Hard Work.............................. 168
The Loyal Man 172
A Life Sentence for Driving While License Revoked 177
Speeding to Court and "Fuzz Busters"..................... 180
The Loosened Tie and the Revealing Dress 186
A Pregnant Juror....................................... 188
The Root Doctor.. 190

PART V: LIFE WITHOUT FATHER............... 193
Their Names are Legion 194
A Probationer's Friend in Lee County 196
The Father Who Showed Back Up 198
Two Marines... 201
The Boy and the Dollar 204

PART VI: A JUDGE ON THE ROAD 207
A Judge's Southern Dinner.............................. 208
Barbecue 211
A Leg Pulled in Warrenton 213
Driving to the Courthouses 217
Mattamuskeet School and the Second Grader............. 221
The Top of the Courthouse............................. 225
A Good Man and the Farmville Christmas Parade 228

PART VII: FINAL THOUGHTS 233
An Oath for the Lawyers 234
Thankful for Justice.................................... 237
A Turtle on a Fence Post............................... 240
Acknowledgments 246

Dedication

Judge John Davis Larkins, Jr., from the small town of Trenton on the Trent River, was a United States District Court Judge for the Eastern District of North Carolina. I clerked for "The Judge" after graduating from Wake Forest Law School in 1974 and passing the bar exam. He was a good man and a good judge, and I always enjoyed being with him in his chambers, driving him to various courthouses, or on duck and goose hunting trips.

The judge's favorite poem, which he could recite by memory, was *Abou Ben Adhem* by Leigh Hunt. I think that the poem expressed what was very important to him, to love his fellow man. As a consequence, Judge Larkins was blessed by the Lord. Below is the poem that he taught me to love:

> *Abou Ben Adhem (may his tribe increase!)*
> *Awoke one night from a deep dream of peace,*
> *And saw, within the moonlight in his room,*
> *Making it rich, and like a lily in bloom,*

CALL YOUR NEXT CASE

An angel writing in a book of gold:—
Exceeding peace had made Ben Adhem bold,
And to the presence in the room he said,
"What writest thou?"—The vision raised its head,
And with a look made of all sweet accord,
Answered, "The names of those who love the Lord."
"And is mine one?" said Abou. "Nay, not so,"
Replied the angel. Abou spoke more low,
But cheerly still; and said, "I pray thee, then,
Write me as one that loves his fellow men."
The angel wrote, and vanished. The next night
It came again with a great wakening light,
And showed the names whom love of God had blest,
And lo! Ben Adhem's name led all the rest.

Foreword

We all have those remarkable days in our lives—those that stand out above all others. The day I was appointed to the bench was such a day in my life. One of the first two people who called to congratulate me was Senior Resident Superior Court Judge W. Russell Duke, Jr. During that brief exchange, Judge Duke expressed his best wishes for my success on the bench. I so appreciated his congratulatory call—even though we did not know each other very well at the time—since the two of us would ultimately serve together in the same judicial district as fellow resident superior court judges.

And that's what can distinguish the judiciary from policy-making venues. Despite different backgrounds, values, and judicial philosophies, judges collectively work together to administer justice. Judge Duke's distinguished twenty-seven-year career as jurist is enough, to be sure, to pique the curiosity of those with an interest in how the process of justice transpires in our courtrooms. But the pearls of wisdom arising from these pages are the reader's real reward.

Judge Duke's distinguished judicial career begins and ends during the last year of two very different presidencies: Ronald Reagan and Barack Obama. No doubt these societal changes loomed large as he administered justice day by day in myriad rural courtrooms. But because W. Russell Duke, Jr. was, in his own words, called to be a judge, he focuses on legal system challenges arising from legal system stakeholders elevating commercialism over professionalism; self-interest over common interest; and unrestrained advocacy over civility. This book appropriately conveys several anecdotes illustrating these concerns. But there are also stories that simply bring joy to the human spirit.

Not only does Judge Duke offer practical insights about the day-to-day challenges and pleasures associated with life on the bench, but he also shares principles that guided his decisions on the bench, including common law, common man, and common sense. Whatever disagreement is engendered among lawyers and judges whenever principles for judicial decision-making are debated, we are all no doubt reminded of the vital role of the judiciary in dispensing equal justice under law.

But above all else, Judge Duke's principal theme centers on the importance of the jury in the operation of our justice system. Though all knowledgeable readers no doubt understand that juries are the exception, not the rule, among the nation-states of our world, Judge Duke reinforces the seminal importance of this institution to the operation of the American justice system. Moreover, the book concludes with an inspiring "Oath of Attorney" for new members of the bar—an oath that he personally administered to new attorneys in his district. The words of this oath leap off the page for those of us who view lawyers as public citizens and servant-leaders with an obligation to promote the cause of justice and serve the needs of their communities.

I was pleased to appoint Judge Duke to the extended faculty at High Point Law. Our law students need to hear his practical observations on judging and lawyering. Without a doubt, Judge Duke gave his best to advance and promote the cause of justice in his generation. I can only hope that we will do the same.

> Chief Justice Mark Martin (fmr)
> Founding Dean and Professor of Law
> Kenneth F. Kahn School of Law at High Point University

CALL YOUR NEXT CASE

PART I: APPROACHING THE BENCH

CALL YOUR NEXT CASE

An Overview of
a Life in Court

In early September of 1971 my first-year law class gathered in the courtroom in Carswell Hall at Wake Forest University School of Law. An oversized portrait of John Marshall, the famous Chief Justice of the United States Supreme Court, stared down at us from the back wall behind the podium.

I sat down on the third row from the back in the oak-paneled hall. The room was beautiful and somewhat intimidating. To get to this courtroom, I had taken the crowded elevator from the basement floor. It being the first day of school, the elevator was full of young men cutting up about the new dean, whom no one really knew. Also on the elevator was a well-dressed man who had a very youthful appearance.

We all exited the elevator into a crowded octagon-shaped lobby with imposing portraits of old men hanging on the walls and made our way to the large, paneled courtroom decorated with Marshall's portrait. When everyone settled down I noticed the young well-dressed man who had been on the elevator. He was sitting comfortably on the podium with other men, one of whom was Dean Carroll Weathers, the veteran dean of the law school. After serving in that role for twenty years, Dean Weathers had retired that spring. As our ethics professor he would impress into our souls the immortal words, "Now, ladies and gentlemen, go out of this school and make a good living; but, more importantly, make a good life."

The young, well-dressed man on the elevator stood to give his first remarks on his first day as the new dean of the law school. And boy, was I glad that I had said nothing on the elevator. I would come to admire Dean Pasco Bowman, who later became a noted judge on the United States Court of Appeals for the Eighth Circuit.

My path to law school began with my father's offhand comment to my mother that if he had it all to do over again he would "get his law license." I was a young boy, and my family was driving to my grandmother's house. With my arms resting on the back of the front seat of my father's Buick Roadmaster, his words became the seed of my desire to become a lawyer. My mind was set.

The process for my admission to law school had begun in the autumn of 1969, the fall semester of my senior year at Wake Forest University. I went over to Carswell Hall to visit with Dean Weathers, a modest, humble, and distinguished lawyer from Raleigh who had been chosen in 1950 to be the dean. He cordially welcomed me and warmly encouraged me to apply after taking the Law School Admission Test.

After taking the LSAT I made my application for admittance to Wake Forest School of Law. Dean Weathers personally interviewed each applicant. In June of 1970, after graduating from Wake Forest, I went again to Dean Weathers' office for my interview. At the close of my interview with the dean and Assistant Dean Leon H. Corbett Jr., Dean Weathers informed me that I was admitted to the 1971 class as a first-year law student.

I worked hard in law school. My professors were all good men who demanded hard work and preparation. With no hint of politics or personal bias, each taught the law. Their very presence inspired me to do my best, and each of them was accessible and encouraging. During the second semester of my second year at the law school I married the love of my life, Patsy Davis.

After graduating from the law school and passing the North Carolina bar exam, I was sworn in as a lawyer in early September of 1974 by Superior Court Judge Robert D. Rouse, Jr. Patsy and I moved to the small town of Trenton, where I went to work as a law clerk for United States District Court Judge John D. Larkins, Jr. Judge Larkins was a great man who had a mild country manner and a wonderful sense of humor. I enjoyed every day that I spent with him for those fifteen months. He was a no-nonsense, fair judge, and I watched him closely. He took me fishing and hunting. We played golf. I listened to every word he said. He encouraged me to be a country lawyer like him.

Upon the completion of my clerkship with Judge Larkins, I opened my law office on Main Street in my hometown of Farmville. My practice expanded. People in my hometown hired me to counsel them in their most important personal and legal matters. It was here in that blessed town that we had our three children and I also became mayor of Farmville.

In my hometown there lived a Superior Court Judge who I had admired all of my life. Judge Robert D. Rouse, Jr., who had sworn me in when I first became a lawyer, was a good man in every respect. He very graciously listened to me and encouraged me in every way. I tried cases before him and I gradually became aware that I wanted to be a judge like him and Judge Larkins. I enjoyed practicing law for fourteen years. In my final four years as a lawyer prior to becoming a judge, I had the opportunity to practice law with Kenneth Hite, a very wise and respected older lawyer in Greenville, our new home. With Mr. Hite's blessing and encouragement, I ran for election as a trial judge and from 1988 until 2016, I enjoyed the best job in the state of North Carolina.

The Judge's Call

I was called to be a judge. A calling seems to me to be any job, occupation, profession, or office to which an individual finds himself led and almost compelled to pursue. The performance of that vocation flows naturally, and most times happily, into the day-to-day pursuit of the right path to follow to get the job done. One must follow his heart in the calling. A person who is called to do a thing is usually not inclined to seek advice or counsel as to which direction to take. The person called often seems to be motivated by some hidden inner force. That person could seem to others to be unfriendly, unwilling to take part in things, not inclined to "play the game."

A trial judge occupies a very lonely position. In the courtroom the trial judge sits on a perch opposite everyone else and is constantly required to make decisions on evidence, procedure, courtroom decorum, and judgment. The judge must make a ruling, applying the law to the facts of the case before him. The trial judge listens to the arguments of lawyers and litigants with a courtroom full of observers, yet the judge, except when assisted by a jury, must hear the matter alone and alone he must rule. Thankfully, most lawyers and litigants who appear before the judge ask only for a fair hearing.

To become a judge in North Carolina a person must be a citizen of the state, over twenty-one years of age, and a licensed attorney. That is the extent of the required qualifications. To be a judge one need not be particularly smart or a star student of the law. In the state of North Carolina a judge must be elected by the voters or appointed by the governor. In 1987 the North Carolina General Assembly created an additional judgeship for the District Court for Judicial District 3, which at that time included Pitt, Craven, Carteret, and Pamlico Counties. In August 1988, after the legislature adjourned their session and left Raleigh, our state capital, I publicly announced that I intended to seek election to the new position in the November election.

At that time the Democratic Party was the dominant party in Eastern North Carolina. For me to be successful, I would need support from most of the Democratic Party's "movers and shakers" in the four counties. Soliciting their support was a pleasurable task. My father was a great help in this endeavor. Because I secured early commitments of support for my candidacy from most of the mayors, legislators, lawyers, clerks, and sheriffs, I was able to run unopposed.

The Big Democrat and the Dog

Campaigning for any office in any party in any precinct, from the most sophisticated one in Baltimore or Chicago to the most primitive one in Bridgetown or La Paz, requires, without exception, touching base with the "movers and shakers" in and around the precinct. It is just the way the world works. Having decided to run in the 1988 election for the office of District Court Judge, my first and most important task was to gain the support of as many of the "movers and shakers" in those four counties as I could. One of the first people who I needed to talk with was Janice Faulkner, a former state treasurer, former head of the North Carolina Division of Motor Vehicles and a strong confidante of former and future Governor James B. Hunt, Jr. Janice was a "mover and shaker."

When I entered her office she was reclined in her obviously very comfortable wingback chair with her bare feet crossed and resting on a small, rather low, footstool in fine needlepoint. She did not budge from her seat and very graciously, with a wonderful smile, asked that I sit down and make myself comfortable. I remember thinking that if I had made myself as comfortable as she appeared, I would soon be in Sleepy Town. After we exchanged some pleasantries she politely began the substantive conversation by asking, "Well my goodness, what can I do for you today?" I then replied that I intended to run for District Court Judge for District 3.

To my chagrin and disappointment, she responded that she admired my ambition but that I was greatly lacking in "name recognition." I looked at her with the confident smile of a happy warrior freshly recruited from the volunteers and said, "Janice, why I probably have more name recognition than anybody in this county." In her serious, yet friendly and pleasant manner, she incredulously asked, "Well now, just how do you figure that?" Matching her seriously friendly and pleasant manner, I answered, "My name is Rusty Duke. *The Reader's Digest* has recently said that the two most used names for dogs are 'Rusty' and 'Duke', and 'Duke' is number one. Now, I ask you, who's going to vote against their dog, their very best friend?" As she chuckled she said, "You know, you might do all right."

Electing Judges and the Bicycle Thief

Two-thirds of U.S. states, including North Carolina, allow their voters to participate in the selection of their judges. The superior court resident judges are elected by the voters in the judicial district in which the judge resides. The candidate for judge must get out on the campaign trail and ask people to vote for him. During the campaign candidates attend forums, often held in churches, to ask for votes and visit with the voters. The candidates deliver a few brief remarks followed by possible questions from those in attendance.

Election of judges is the fairest and most transparent method of selecting judges. Generally speaking, the voters make an honest effort to secure some information about the candidates from local newspapers, lawyers and judges, social media, campaign literature, and neighbors. The alternative method for selection of judges in North

Carolina is to let the politicians do it. First, we could have appointment by the governor. The governor might rely on input from local and statewide political contributors, big law firms, law professors and special interest groups. Many of the members of these special interest groups look on the ordinary citizens as simple-minded people clinging to their guns and Bibles, incapable of contributing anything worthwhile except a few taxes.

Many sophisticated people would say that the smartest and more propitious method of selecting judges is what is called the "merit selection" process. These people will proclaim that this method "gets rid of the politics." Be assured that people on the merit selection commission would be political contributors, members of big law firms, law professors, and members in very good standing of special interest groups. If forced, maybe the commission organizers will allow one or two ordinary citizens to serve on the panel. Whether the candidate possesses enough merit to be a judge would seem to be a very subjective measure on which to rely, but a more important question may be whether he feels called to be a judge.

Requiring judges to be selected by election forces the ones who would be our judges to get out and subject themselves to examination by the ordinary citizens, as well as the special interest groups and associations, big law firms, money people, law professors, and anyone else interested in the administration of justice. The "good ole boys" would not be excluded; however, they don't get to be the sole voice in the selection either. Most people would agree that political campaigning educates the public about the candidate. Conversely, and most importantly, political campaigning educates the candidate about the people.

In 2000 I was reelected to a second full eight-year term as one of two resident Superior Court Judges for Judicial District 3A, Pitt County. In that race, four people were running for two judgeships. The two incumbent judges were reelected. During the campaign all the candidates had several opportunities to attend candidate forums, church suppers, teas, parties, and volunteer fireman fundraisers and eat a lot of barbeque pig and chicken.

A Baptist church in west Greenville held a candidate forum which the other candidates for judge and I attended. After I made my short remarks, a young man about twenty-five to thirty years old rose to complain and announced, "Judge Duke gave a man an active sentence of thirty days for stealing a bicycle." The man was very emotional and excited. He said that I was not fair and was far too heavy-handed.

When the young man finished speaking, I indicated from my seat in the audience that I would like to respond to the remarks that he had made. The church was full. I recalled the case, rose from my seat, and said something like the following: "During the sentencing hearing of the man who pled guilty to stealing the bicycle, I learned that the victim was the twelve-year-old child of a man who collects garbage for the City of Greenville. The child's father was at the hearing in the lower court, having been excused from work to attend and testify. The defendant had appealed the misdemeanor after having been found guilty in the District Court."

I continued, "Not long before I heard the case, my oldest son's bright yellow bicycle had been stolen. When my son, who was about the same age as the victim in the case, looked up at me with his blue eyes and reported that his bicycle had been stolen, I knew for sure that I could promise my son that I would get him another bicycle. On the other hand, that father might not be able to look into his son's brown eyes and assure him that he could get him a new bicycle. A new bicycle was a bigger bite out of his paycheck than out of mine. Now, yes, I gave the defendant thirty days in jail, and I would do so again. People want what little property they may have to be left alone and not taken by someone who could get out and work and buy his own bicycle." After I finished my remarks I received a hearty applause from a very warm audience. All people deserve and should expect equal justice under the law. And all people deserve an opportunity to see and question a person who wants to be their judge.

The Most Enjoyable Job

I was sworn in on the morning of the first Monday in December in 1988. The Chief District Court Judge for Judicial District 3 assigned me to the criminal court of Craven County beginning that very same morning and continuing for the rest of the week. That was it. No training. For the next two years, I earned a reputation for being a tough, no-nonsense judge in traffic court, family court and child support court.

In 1989 the North Carolina General Assembly created an additional judgeship for the Superior Court for Judicial District 3A, Pitt County. After the new Superior Court judgeship was created, several lawyers and others asked me if I was interested in seeking that position. My initial response was that I did not think I was inclined to run. Upon encouragement from an older, more experienced District Court Judge, an old friend of my father's who had been a very influential legislator before becoming a judge, I changed my mind. In August of 1989, after the legislature adjourned their session and left Raleigh, I publicly announced that I intended to seek election to the new Superior court position in the November 1990 election.

As the January 1990 two-week filing period approached, it appeared that I may not have any opposition, but by the time the two weeks had passed a retired District Court Judge and an assistant district attorney had also filed for election. The three of us were Democrats, so the election would be determined in the May Democratic Party primary election. When all the counting had been completed, my opponents had received about fifty percent of the vote between them and I received about fifty percent, making me a newly elected Superior Court Judge for Judicial District 3A, Pitt County. My swearing-in would take place the first day of January in 1991. From May until the following January, I continued to hold court in the district court of the four counties of Judicial District 3.

At the January 1991 ceremony, held in the remodeled 1968 Pitt County Superior court courtroom, the Clerk of Superior Court of Pitt County swore me in as a Resident Superior Court Judge. In our county there were two Superior Court Judges and, since the other judge was there before me, by seniority he held the position of Senior Resident Superior Court Judge.

As a general jurisdiction trial judge, the most serious criminal and civil cases would come before me. I would be one of just over one hundred Superior Court Judges in our state. It would be my task to hold superior court in the counties assigned to me by the Chief Justice of the Supreme Court of North Carolina. I held court on weekly terms and would be assigned for six-month assignments to judicial districts made up of from one to as many as seven counties.

I considered this the most enjoyable job anyone could hold in the judicial system; even better, I considered it the most pleasurable endeavor in the whole of the world. Every day my job could be aptly described, to borrow a phrase attributed to Mrs. Gump, "like a box of chocolates," with me not knowing what was coming next. Living the life of my calling would be one magnificent and joyful honor. This favorable chance to serve the great people of North Carolina as a trial judge filled me with gratitude to them for their trust. The opportunity to be their agent, to administer their majestic and powerful law, filled me with respect and reverence for the people. I simply love the people, the common man, the jurors.

The Days in the Life of a Superior Court Judge

During the time that I served as a Superior Court Judge, North Carolina was divided into eight judicial divisions. The judicial divisions were each divided into judicial districts, and across the state there were thirty-nine judicial districts. As the days pass and new political relationships form, the judicial districts evolve along those boundaries chosen through politics in the counties and the state.

For local political reasons in the four counties, the Pitt County district attorney wanted to peel off Pitt County and that was done. Not so many sessions of the General Assembly later, the Superior Court Judges were attracted to having two districts, and Pitt County became Judicial District 3A for the district attorneys and the Superior Court Judges. The District Court Judges were elected in the four counties of Judicial District 3 when I first ran in 1988. The next election saw the District Court Judges become two separate judicial districts.

After fifty or so years as a lawyer and a judge, I am persuaded that we have the fairest and most just criminal justice system in the world today. It has evolved over the past millennium from the English Common Law. The objective and fair-minded application of criminal justice in our state and our nation rests on the people, the bedrock foundation that a jury of our peers shall determine the facts of our case and declare our guilt. The process is public and reviewable by appellate courts. The law does not require that an accused person have a perfect trial, only that the defendant have a trial free of prejudicial error.

Campaigning for public office is a pleasure. Meeting new people and forming new friendships is a very beneficial byproduct of the electioneering process, especially since the candidate has an opportunity to meet some very interesting people who live in vastly different situations and circumstances.

During my first campaign my wife and I were guests of friends who had hired a man to help with the guests during the party. I struck up a conversation with the man, who was in his late sixties or seventies. He knew that I was running for judge. He told me how he and his wife had to padlock themselves inside their home after dark in order to sleep. The old man described to me how thugs more or less ruled the streets and the neighborhood by sheer intimidation. He related to me how he and his wife used to be fond of sitting on their front porch, but with the unrestrained urination and cursing around their home, that was no longer enjoyable or even possible. This conversation had a huge impact on me. This man and his wife deserved, as citizens of our community, state, and nation, to have the same peace and enjoyment of their home that my wife and I experienced in our neighborhood.

In all of our elections to various offices, from the agricultural agent at the bottom of the ballot to the President of the United States at the top, the people, the voters, can learn much about the candidates running for a particular office. Ironically and even more importantly, the candidate learns about the people and their different situations and circumstances. If the candidate's heart is "in the right place" then his love and admiration for the people and their will is stimulated and grows. However, those politicians whose hearts are focused on their own personal needs for popularity and gain and their own reelection come to cynically deplore the people. The smarter these politicians think they are and the greater esteem they feel for themselves, the more contempt they have for the people.

The people of the community, the county in which I found myself judging on any given day, were very important to me. The common law, the common man, and common sense inspired me in every courtroom in which I presided. It was the common jury that awakened my sense of respect for the people daily. I never felt at home in any courthouse without a jury somewhere in the building. Every step I took was taken out of a deep respect and admiration for the people, for their interest in their county courthouse and the justice for which it stood.

Perhaps the most important duty that a judge has is to fairly and impartially, that is, without prejudice, sentence and punish a convicted person. In the process of sentencing defendants who pled guilty or were convicted of a crime by a jury, I considered first, the nature of the crime; second, the record and demeanor of the defendant; third, the circumstances of the victim, if a victim was affected; and fourth, the community and the right of the residents of the neighborhood to enjoy their property and have some sort of peace. Oftentimes, as I considered a matter before me, I would wonder in my mind, "What would the community have me do in this case?"

My typical day would begin with the five-minute drive from my home to the Pitt County Courthouse, an hour-or-so drive to some county seat like Goldsboro, or a two-hour drive to Manteo in Dare County. Each Resident Judge would be assigned to a judicial district, and the county or counties within that district, for a term of six months. The drive to the neighboring counties in our Judicial Division would be along lonely back roads in eastern North Carolina.

Most mornings and evenings on return trips home, the drive would consist of just admiring the beautiful scenery. Occasionally I would be treated to sights of deer, turkeys, or a bear.

At all the county courthouses—the larger more populated counties such as Wilson, Goldsboro or Wilmington and the smaller counties such as Gates, Chowan, or Hyde—I would be greeted by a bailiff upon my arrival. The bailiff would usually be a county sheriff's deputy who I knew. He would greet me cheerfully with a warm smile and grab my book bag or anything I might attempt to carry.

The first time that I went to Gatesville, the county seat of Gates County, I was greeted in the front of the courthouse by this rather short, stocky, jolly, fellow in a typical brown sheriff's deputy's uniform. He grabbed my book bags out of the boot of my car while I grabbed my robe. While walking the short distance to the front door, I asked him how everything was going and the two of us exchanged pleasantries. I then asked him how the High Sheriff was doing and he, to my great surprise, exclaimed, "Why Judge, I am the High Sheriff!" This fine elected sheriff was humbly carrying my bags. I was a little bit embarrassed and would have retrieved my bags if he had let me.

When I arrived one morning in Goldsboro, the Wayne County Courthouse was surrounded by TV trucks with their antennae stretching higher than the courthouse roof.

My bailiff, Mr. Harvell, came out of the courthouse to greet me and help me with my bags. I asked him about the TV trucks and he very quickly began to tell me about the capital murder case that would begin that morning. We would shortly begin the jury selection for a double murder trial that would last for the next few weeks. As with each case called by the District attorney from the trial calendar, simply arriving at a county courthouse would bring an occasional surprise.

Advice to a Young Judge

Superior Court Judges are "circuit judges". The judges hold court in a judicial district on a set six-month rotation schedule. The court convenes on a weekly term in the county or various counties in the judicial district. The weekly term within the six-month rotation schedule is a very good arrangement for placing judges into service, because a five-day work week often fits well with the length of trials and the schedules of lawyers.

Judges do not stay in one court or county too long and thus do not have the opportunity to develop friendships that could appear to be bothersome to others. North Carolina has experienced almost no judicial misconduct or wrongdoing, and this is due in no small part to the arrangement and the implementation of judicial resources.

One afternoon in the spring of 1991 I stopped in Farmville to visit Judge Robert Rouse, a retired Superior Court Judge who was sick and dying of cancer. This judge had known me since I was five or six years old and was a good friend of my father's. Sitting in his den, with a painting of Normandy's Utah Beach over the mantle, we talked about the life of a judge. The judge had been known and respected throughout the state and had run his court in a no-nonsense, get-the-job-done manner, unintentionally causing some of the judges with a less rigorous work ethic to be a bit uncomfortable.

My father had always spoken very highly of Judge Rouse, and over the years I came to also hold the judge in high regard and considered him a treasured mentor. As a lawyer I had tried cases before him. He had shown confidence in me when he appointed me to represent a young man charged with first-degree rape. As our visit was ending and I was rising to leave, I asked him if he had any advice for a young inexperienced judge. He replied that two things came to his mind. "First," he said, "don't ever give a reason for a ruling from the bench. It only invites cross-examination. The lawyers will say to you, 'Well judge, have you thought of this, that or the other?'" He emphatically added, "You don't want that."

"Please tell me your other advice to a young judge," I asked. Then the judge warned me that lawyers and other court personnel would tell me how very smart I was, how such and such thing I did or ruling I made was so great and how knowledgeable I was. With a stern countenance he looked at me and said, "The moment that you start to believe them is the moment that you begin your walk down a fool's road." Within six short weeks the judge would be gone. I never saw Judge Rouse again after our visit in his den and I have never forgotten his wise words.

Over the following years I would notice "man's empty praise" and those making the offering. In response I would usually let them know that they were mighty kind to say such things, but in my heart I knew that they were only courting with their own considered objective in mind.

The Ruling is Final

My maternal grandmother, who we called Mema, was a happy jovial woman who always wore a smile and just shook when she laughed, which was often. At times she would pronounce that one thing or another was the way it was or was going to be. There was no use in arguing with her after the ruling had been made. To give whatever she had said added authority, she would proclaim that the answer she had given was all in accordance with the law of the Medes and Persians, which could not be repealed. We had no clue who the Medes and Persians were, but we figured that they must be important. Quoting Darius, she would reverently invoke the King James Bible and declare with a smile, "The thing is true, according to the law of the Medes and Persians, which altereth not."

Following Mema's good-humored and self-assured example, it was unusual for me to change a ruling after it was made. Judge Rouse had counseled me to avoid explaining my rulings. It was against the rules and so very seldom that a lawyer would continue his argument after my decision was pronounced. My fixed and firm resolution must have been the consequence of my training in the law the Medes and Persians. I was appreciably mindful of the blessing that my ruling was subject to review by a higher court in Raleigh. There the judges gather together with the assistance of a cadre of law clerks. There in that hallowed hall the judges, at their pleasure, would carefully review my ruling. They would either uphold it, alter it, or reverse it, all in accordance with the law, not of the Medes and Persians, but the State of North Carolina.

PART II:
Taking Care of Business

Order in the Court

Bailiffs are special friends of judges. The courtroom bailiffs are the arms and legs of the judge. The bailiff is the herald of the court, the court crier. My first terms of superior court in Pitt County were held in the spring of 1991. Mr. Withers Harvey, the retired county coroner, was one of my bailiffs. Deputy Robert Hudson from Black Jack, a Pitt County township, was my other bailiff, assisted by Harold Evans. Deputies Hudson and Evans were armed, but I never observed Mr. Harvey carrying a pistol. Mr. Harvey was a quiet and distinguished gentleman. He always wore a dark suit and an appropriate tie. He was a tall, slender man with a serious, yet friendly, countenance. Mr. Harvey, as we always called him, was some thirty years my senior.

Before becoming a judge my abiding respect for the common citizen made me want to start court promptly, at the very minute of the scheduled time. Mr. Harvey felt the same way. With Mr. Harvey there it was literally embarrassing to be a minute late opening court. He was a noble man. As the appointed time to open court approached, if I by chance was in chambers talking with lawyers, Mr. Harvey would come get me. He would not knock on the door to the chambers; on the contrary, Mr. Harvey would enter boldly and announce that the time for opening court was nigh. We all would rise and leave the judge's chambers to walk toward the courtroom. It was not too long before lawyers and those having business before the court realized that they could set their watches by the time of the opening of Judge Duke's court.

With Mr. Harvey opening court on time in his dignified manner, a palpable air of "taking care of business" was brought to the courtroom. The entire court day was more orderly since it began in an orderly manner. A step ahead of the judge, Mr. Harvey would take the lead into the courtroom. As he walked within the bar from the courtroom's entrance door to the bench he would announce in a strong and authoritative voice, "All rise." About seven or eight paces into the courtroom he would stop. The courtroom would grow very quiet and all movement would cease. Mr. Harvey would allow the calm to settle in and then he would look at me. At a slight nod from me he would open court for the day in a voice heard throughout the large room, "Oh yes, oh yes, oh yes, this Superior Court for the County of Pitt is now open for the dispatch of business with the Honorable

W. Russell Duke, Jr., Judge presiding. God save this State and this Honorable Court. You may be seated." It was a prayer that I cherished. I loved the courtroom and I loved Mr. Harvey.

From the calling of the case until the acceptance of the verdict, and the sentencing hearing following the verdict, if needed, the average criminal jury trial would take me about a day-and-a-half to try. The actual proceeding would begin with an order addressed to the prosecutor to call his next case. The prosecutor would respond by saying, "The State calls 'The State of North Carolina versus Joe Jones.' Come around Mr. Jones." Twelve jurors would then be called at random from the jury pool and seated in their assigned seats in the jury box. The remaining members of the jury pool would stay in the courtroom, and then my introduction of the case would begin. I would introduce the twelve jurors in the box to the defendant and his lawyer and inform them of the charge or charges against the defendant, then introduce them to the lawyers for the state and the alleged victim, if any, of the crime charged. After these introductions, I would outline to them how the case would proceed.

The lawyers for both the defendant and the state would proceed through the jury selection and find twelve jurors and usually an alternate to serve as the jury. The jury would then be impaneled, and the trial would begin. Once you impanel a jury, you cannot end the trial except by a verdict or a mistrial. The lawyers then give their opening statements to the jury, giving the jury panel an outline of what the lawyers believe the competent and admissible evidence will show in the case.

The opening statements are usually very brief, and they are not the time to argue the case. On occasion a lawyer might stray away from a simple outline of his idea of what the facts may be and drift off course into argument. He would be politely interrupted the first time, not so politely interrupted the second time, and instructed to sit down should a third violation of the rule occur.

After the opening statements are given to the jury, the state is invited to call its first witness and the presentation of evidence begins. The bailiff would offer the Bible before the witness and, unless the witness requested to be affirmed without the Bible, the witness would place his left hand on the Bible and raise his right hand. The courtroom clerk or the judge would ask, "Do you promise (sometimes, "swear") to tell the truth, the whole truth and nothing but the truth, so help you God?" The affirmation differs only in that the witness "affirms" to tell the truth and is asked at the end of the affirmation, "Is this your solemn affirmation?" Upon an affirmative answer to the question, the bailiff asks the witness to take his seat in the witness chair. The witness would then answer the state's lawyer's questions and then be submitted to cross-examination by the defendant's lawyer.

Upon the call and testimony of the first witness, the trial and presentation of evidence proceeds until the state's prosecuting lawyer announces to the court that there are no further state's witnesses or no further evidence for the state and says, "The State of North Carolina rests (or rests its case)," At that point, before the jury, I would look at the lawyer for the defendant and ask, "Is there any evidence for the defendant?" The lawyer for the defendant would answer either "yes" or "no." Should the defendant's lawyer answer "No," then the presentation of the evidence in the case is complete. If the defendant's lawyer has stated that there would be evidence for the defendant, then I would say to him, "You may call your first witness." The lawyer would call the first witness and, in the same manner as the state's witnesses, the witness would be sworn or affirmed, answer the defendant's lawyer's questions and then be submitted to be cross-examined by the state's lawyer.

When the defendant has called all his witnesses and offered all the evidence he intends to present to the jury, the lawyer for the defendant would announce before the jury that all of the evidence for the defendant has been presented and "the defendant rests." I would then look at the state's lawyer and ask, "Is there anything further from the state?" The prosecutor understands that now is the opportunity for the state to offer any rebuttal to the defendant's evidence through witnesses. The state may offer evidence in the same manner as it initially presented the evidence, or it may decline to offer any further evidence. If no rebuttal evidence is offered, then the prosecutor would announce that there would be nothing further from the state. The presentation of evidence to the jury would then be complete.

Next, the jury is informed by the judge that all of the evidence has been presented and that soon it would be their duty to consider and examine the evidence, apply the law as I would give them to apply in the case, and arrive at their verdict. The jury would be told that I must hold a hearing outside of their presence to confer with the lawyers as to the law that would apply to the case, and then they would be excused from the courtroom.

After I had informed the lawyers of the law that would be given to the jury for them to apply to the evidence, the jury, having returned to the courtroom, would then hear the closing arguments of the lawyers for both the state and the defendant. Upon completion of the closing arguments of the lawyers, I would instruct the jury on all of the law that they should apply to the evidence in the case. The jury is then instructed to "find the true facts of the case and render or return a verdict reflecting the truth as they, the jury, find it to be."

Control of the Courtroom

When I was serving as a judge, after the call of the calendar the criminal trial week would begin by my looking at the district attorney and saying, "Call your first case." The defendant, who was called and who had just answered "present" at the calendar call, would come forward with his lawyer meeting him at the defense table. At that time I would ask, "Do we need a jury?" If the reply was that a jury was not necessary and that the defendant planned to enter a plea of guilty, a plea and sentencing hearing would usually follow.

It has been my profound experience that almost all criminal defendants accept without protest the punishment imposed by the court. Most convicted defendants have a deep respect for the administration of justice and completely understand that they deserve the penalty. In their heart they understand that justice is rendering one his due, that for the court to impose a lesser punishment than deserved merits their scorn and lack of respect. On the other hand, the imposition of a greater punishment than that deserved diminishes the defendant's respect for the rule of law and produces an unquiet insolence toward the governing authority.

My aim was to be fair – fair to the convicted defendant, fair to the victim, if any, and fair to the community. A just judge is called upon to carefully weigh on the scales of justice the considerations of each party. Too much punishment for the defendant is an embarrassment to the victim, and too little a cause for disdain. During his tenure a judge can bring great respect and approval to the courts, or just scatter the high regard and honor for the court as chaff in the wind. He has to watch what he is doing.

CALL YOUR NEXT CASE

Lawyer Tough and Breakfast at McDonald's

As the summer of 1993 approached, I had now been "on the bench," a trial judge, for a little over two years. I was now the Senior Resident Superior Court Judge for Pitt County. Since January of 1991, I had held civil and criminal court in Pitt County and about ten other counties in the eastern part of the state. It would be my duty to hear civil or criminal cases, and sometimes both, during weekly terms in the counties of the district to which I was assigned by the Chief Justice of the Supreme Court of North Carolina.

Civil cases are matters and controversies primarily arising out of contracts and torts, mostly personal injuries. Civil sessions involve hearing motions on Monday morning and calling the trial docket set for the week. Each of the cases are called by the presiding judge from a calendar prepared by the judicial district's senior resident judge.

Civil motions hearings are attended by lawyers prepared to argue specific motions. Litigants or parties to the case, plaintiffs and defendants, would very seldom need to be present. The motions would involve discovery issues, motions to compel one side or the other to give to the opponent information that is "discoverable" under the rules of discovery. The motion may be one where a lawyer seeks to withdraw as counsel for the plaintiff or the defendant. There are various motions for the judge to hear. The most consequential motions would be those asking for dismissal of the other side's case, a motion to dismiss or motion for summary judgment. Whether the judge's decision was in their favor or not, most lawyers are grateful to have a fair hearing and satisfied that a decision had been made.

Plaintiff's cases, especially those based on personal injury claims, are many times taken on a contingency fee arrangement between the client and the lawyer. That means that, unless the client recovers some monetary settlement, the lawyer does not get paid for his time and effort. Because of this, some lawyers who represent plaintiffs in personal injury claims seem to take on an air of saintliness and moral zeal, exposing their presumption that their case should not be hindered to any degree and certainly not dismissed.

These lawyers seem to be convinced that the law of the land should be expanded to take in their client's case, and that the defendants ought to expect this expansion of the law.

Due to the adversarial nature of our system, those who primarily represent the plaintiffs and those who choose to defend don't welcome or appreciate rulings inconsistent with their position. Most lawyers are of the opinion that a judge who commendably rules in their favor is truly a smart judge. To rule against them, as they see things, shows a distinct lack of attention or understanding.

I find wisdom in Abraham Lincoln's advice to lawyers, written in 1850: "Discourage litigation. Persuade your neighbors to compromise whenever you can. Point out to them how the nominal winner is often a real loser – in fees, expenses, and waste of time. As a peacemaker the lawyer has a superior opportunity of being a good man. There will still be business enough."

Advertising encourages litigation. People now subconsciously regard every person they meet on the highways and streets, and parking lots, as customers and patrons, patients and clients, all are now potential plaintiffs who have been encouraged, not discouraged, by lawyers to sue them. People are actually being encouraged by lawyers to look for a wrong that just maybe will award them a fee taken from money out of some other citizen's pocket or insurance company.

To engage in advertising demeans the lawyer and his profession. It was in the middle of the 1970s when the Supreme Court of the United States struck down the rule of professional conduct prohibiting advertising by lawyers.

This was an era that saw that court excitedly enthralled in social engineering. Advertising is now condoned by the state. Advertising has hurt our profession and done even more harm to the fabric of community in our state and nation by pitting neighbor against neighbor.

When I graduated from law school in 1974, lawyers were not allowed to advertise their services. People who needed the services of a lawyer would find the lawyer with the best reputation in their community. Three years later the U.S. Supreme Court, relying upon data supplied by the most prominent lawyer trade association, the American Bar Association, ruled that the prohibition of advertising by lawyers was a violation of commercial free speech.

This ruling fundamentally transformed the legal profession into just another commercial enterprise. For many lawyers, the license to practice law became a vehicle to chase after clients, with the hope and thrill of making lots of money rather than advising and guiding people who found themselves in need of legal advice. Accidents and acts of potential negligence became sources of insurance money to "share" with the injured. For some lawyers, the courtroom became the center of a commercial enterprise rather than a temple of justice. The popularity of the legal profession dropped below that of used car sales.

Lawyer Tough was a "friend." He was a plaintiff's lawyer who unabashedly advertised and actively sought employment in personal injury cases. He and his partner employed several young lawyers who would be sent forth to push the case through the court to seek an early settlement and avoid trial if possible. By spring of 1993 I had ruled on two of Lawyer Tough's cases in two different counties, and both rulings had been very disappointing to Lawyer Tough.

In early summer of 1993 Lawyer Tough called to invite me to have breakfast with him at McDonald's. On the following Friday we met at McDonald's, stood in line, and ordered breakfast.

Having ordered first, I sat down at a three-person orange table and he joined me, sitting in the space closest to me. It was a small table and seemed to me to be a bit close. He began the conversation by telling me that he had consulted with his father about some sort of message that his fellow lawyers felt a need to convey to me. He then, assuring me that he was my friend, smiled and said, "I hope that you don't shoot the messenger." With amusement I assured him that my pistol was outside in my Mercury (although I didn't have one) and that he need not give it another thought.

My friend began to tell me about how there was a lot of talk among the lawyers about my performance as senior resident judge, how disappointed lawyers were, and on and on, and how two lawyers had each pledged twenty-five thousand dollars to elect my opponent in the next election. He went on to say, "Oh my goodness, the campaign would cost one hundred thousand dollars to win in the next judge's race. Do you really want to go through all that?" I listened. I said nothing.

When he had finally finished talking I said, "You say you're my friend. And I appreciate your coming to me with this word of warning." I thanked him for his friendship. He expressed to me how grateful he was that I was listening and thanked me for how I was so open. Then I said to him, "I need to know if I can trust you to take a word back to the lawyers you told me about." He responded that he would be glad to tell them whatever I told him. I then asked, "Verbatim?" He answered twice, "Yes, I will tell them verbatim what you say."

Then I looked him straight in his eyes and said, "Tell them this verbatim. I will continue to do what I think is right by the law. Period. And, if they don't like it and I want to run for reelection, then I will match their one hundred thousand dollars and anything else they want to put on the table. Please tell them that for me." That was a big stretch, but he didn't doubt my determination. He seemed to be a bit taken aback. Of course, I knew that there were no others and that he was just, in his coarse fashion, trying to throw his weight around. We parted amicably and I never heard another negative peep out of him. Commercial enterprise had thrown professionalism out on its hind end. And, so far as I know, he is still my friend.

Attention to the Court

In my fourteen years of practicing law in Pitt and Greene Counties before I became a judge, it was my opportunity and pleasure to observe the different judges before whom I appeared and how they conducted their courts. In the English tradition we have named our law courts with the same word as the kings have named their domain: "Courts." It was my observation that the judges who gained the most respect from the public and from lawyers were those who opened their courts on the designated hour and remained on the bench to take care of the business of the court in an orderly and judicious manner.

The judge sets the tone of the room. He is to conduct himself with authority in a gracious manner. The judge's presence should summon respect, and oftentimes fear. The trial judge is placed on a lofty perch, to sit on a bench conspicuously placed in the center of a large and majestic room. A trial judge is expected to conduct himself in a judicious manner and with a gracious spirit. The presence of a trial judge, especially in the courtroom, should certainly summon to men's hearts respect and a healthy fear of the law.

"Punctuality is the politeness of kings," says the Count of Monte Cristo in Alexandre Dumas' famous book. Opening court on time, at the appointed hour, sets the tone of authority and attention to the court that the law and the people deserve. The judge's task is to do the business before the court. As a law clerk for a federal judge, it was my duty to call his court into session with the words, "All those having business before this Court are to draw nigh, give attention, and ye shall be heard." Punctuality exhibits respect for the people in court, the clerks, and other co-workers of the judge. It also indicates the reliability of the judge, organization of the court system, and a sense of professionalism. Punctuality enhances the reputation of the judge and the courthouse.

A judge should attend to the business of the court. He owes his service to the docket and should concentrate his attention to the matters before him with mindfulness, thoughtfulness, and his thorough concentration. The case before him at any given time deserves nothing less than his full scrutiny and regard. The judge's full allegiance to this duty reveals his respect for the law, the legal process, and the people.

CALL YOUR NEXT CASE

Completing The Docket

A fundamental characteristic of our legal system is the district attorney's executive function of calling criminal cases for trial. A problem arises when the district attorney cannot fill a week with cases to call before the court. Because district attorneys have to face the public in elections and lawyers are talked about by the man on the street, the most effective action by a judge to get things done and force the call of cases is to seat the jury pool in the courtroom with him. The judge should seek to keep the jury as close to him as possible, never letting them out of his sight.

In the presence of the jury, made up of taxpayers and voters who are almost always working people, things happen. When the judge looks down at the district attorney, the prosecutor, and says, "Call your next case," the taxpayers and voters are watching, literally at his back, almost looking over his shoulder, expecting something to happen. And it does. Lawyers scurry and clients come forward to either plead to something or plead "not guilty" and pick a jury of twelve from the jury pool.

In January of 1994 circumstances placed me in Pitt County to hold court for the entire year. Ordinarily any individual judge would be scheduled to hold one six-month term in one county before moving to another county. At the beginning of 1994 the Pitt County criminal docket had a little over 2,100 criminal cases pending in the superior court. In 1994, before the renovations and additions to the Pitt County courthouse, there was no "jury pool room." A jury pool room is where the jury goes to "cool its heels" while the judge, the district attorney and the lawyers slowly work their cases in the courtroom. Since there was no jury poolroom in the courthouse, the jury had to sit in the courtroom.

With the jury present in the courtroom, the threat of a jury trial was always present. But without the jury in the courtroom to watch the proceedings, things seemed to slow down and many cases seemed to be continued. The docket was large and the county jail was full of defendants charged with various crimes, but there seemed to be little urgency to move the cases to plea or to trial. The prosecutor seemed hesitant as he called the unsettled cases, since he truly didn't know what might happen. The atmosphere changed with a jury pool in the courtroom.

The number-one requirement for any lawyer when entering a courtroom is to be prepared. A judge just needs to know how to try a case, any case; however, a lawyer must need to be prepared to try his client's case. This is a rule for both the prosecutor and the defense lawyer. When lawyers realize that there is a real possibility that a case might be called and that they will be called upon to do something in the case besides find a way to continue it, they come to the courtroom prepared.

This climate is created by the judge. If the judge likes to work and if he loves to try cases, then lawyers prepare. If the judge cannot stand the notion of being reversed by the appellate court or likes to fish or hunt, then the cases stand a good chance of being settled by a very liberal plea bargain or being continued. All the lawyers know the judge's work ethic and demeanor and have heard of his yearning to be free to fish or hunt, or his thoughts of home or office, or his propensity to be any place other than the courtroom. Whether he acknowledges it or not, the judge's work is to be present and attentive and prepared to try cases and fairly administer justice.

The first week of 1994 commenced my third year as a Superior Court Judge. The Pitt County jail was full of defendants awaiting the hearing of their cases. Periodically the administrative office of the courts would send me several pages linked together at the bottom and top, with perforated holes in the side that one could peel off. The docket numbers of the cases were printed on the pages with no names, just the numbers and no other information.

In the first weeks of January I assured the district attorney that he had a judge who was willing to work with him. At that time I had shared with no one my goal of trying to significantly reduce the Pitt County criminal docket. It was a worthy goal, and one that I knew we could accomplish. We had a well-regarded district attorney in Pitt County and he had some hard-working young assistants. This was going to be fun. All I had to do was be there and just say the magic words, "Call your next case."

After about three or four weeks, using every available day of the weekly terms, the district attorney came across the courthouse to visit me. I had pasted on a wall in my office the perforated sheets of white paper with the Pitt County criminal docket. When he came into my office, there was the posted docket. I could tell that he had heard a report from someone that I had posted his docket, because he asked me, "What's this, Pard?" I responded, "That's your docket, all your pending cases officially from the administrative office of the courts in Raleigh."

We had a nice visit. Neither of us had to say anything about the situation. We both knew the rules. We were both constitutional officers and it was he who was in charge of the criminal docket. I knew that he was smart. I knew that he was a hard worker. I knew that he had good assistants in his office who would work. And I knew that he had a healthy regard for the citizens and voters of Pitt County.

The job and my goal would get done. By the spring of 1995 the Pitt County criminal docket had been trimmed by about two-thirds, to a grand total of a little over 700 cases.

We'll Pick a Jury at Two o'clock

When I took my first oath as a Superior Court Judge on January 1, 1991, Pitt County scheduled seventeen sessions of superior civil court. In those seventeen weekly sessions, civil cases were given priority. The week's session would begin on Monday with civil motions, and civil jury trials would take priority for the remainder of the week, with the final days of the week reserved for non-jury civil matters.

The jurors would be summoned to appear for duty at two o'clock on the Monday of the week's term. On the Monday of a weekly court, both civil and criminal terms, the court would convene at ten o'clock and remain in session until all business before the court had been completed.

At a civil session the week would begin with the calling and hearing of civil motions. Usually, litigants did not appear in court to hear the civil motions, and the courtroom would be crowded with lawyers representing either the plaintiffs or the defendants waiting for the hearing of the motions in their cases. To avoid wasting the jurors' time, any motions not heard on Monday morning would be heard later in the week. The first jury trial would be called for trial at two o'clock Monday afternoon and would begin with the selection of a jury. The second case on the docket would be called at the completion of the first civil case, and so on.

Early on I earned the reputation of enjoying trying cases before a jury. Working with a jury and with good lawyers gave me great pleasure. The prospect of a case being appealed very seldom entered my mind. My job was to provide a fair and impartial forum in which to try cases. For some lawyers it is a difficult thing to release control of their client's case and place the resolution of the conflict in the hands of a jury. When lawyers found themselves in my court, they could be almost certain that the case would be tried to a verdict by a jury and that preparation for trial was the number-one priority.

On one occasion, after hearing some motions in a civil matter on the trial docket, the lawyers for each side followed me to my chambers and asked if they could talk with me about the case. As I was taking my seat at my desk, one of the lawyers said to me, "Judge, I know that you can help us settle this case." I knew both of the lawyers and have a lot of respect for both. And as honest as each of them were,

I knew that each would explain to their respective client that the case was settled by following the guidance and recommendation of the judge.

I looked at each of the lawyers and said, "Weren't both of you in the same law class? You've known each other for years, right? This case is two years old. You've had plenty of time to talk with one another about the case. You've been through discovery. It appears that the mediation hearing was conducted. And now, you're asking me to help you settle the case?" They both nodded their heads. I looked at each of them and said, "At two o'clock we're going to pick a jury of twelve citizens, tried and true, who are going to tell us all about this case." They smiled and got up and left my office. At the call of the case for trial that afternoon they both rose to announce the case had settled. The following case on the docket was called for trial.

There were very few times when the lawyers were not prepared to try their case. One such time was at a regularly scheduled civil term of court in Pitt County. As with all such sessions, the week began on Monday morning with the hearing of motions. At this weekly term a former judge, now practicing law, moved to continue his client's case from the trial docket. The lawyer representing the defendant, the one being sued, objected. The lawyer for the defendant was a very experienced lawyer and a member of one of the better firms in Pitt County.

After the plaintiff's lawyer had been heard regarding the motion to continue the trial, I then heard the defendant's lawyer. The defendant's lawyer pointed out that the case had some age on it and had been continued three times before by different judges. He pointed out that he was prepared to try the case and persuasively contended that further delay would be prejudicial to the defendant. He asked that I deny the plaintiff's motion to continue. I considered the matter and, having heard from each of the lawyers, I denied the motion to continue and told the lawyers that we would begin the selection of the jury at two o'clock that afternoon.

That motion was the last one scheduled that morning, so court was recessed until two o'clock that afternoon. I left the bench and courtroom to go to my office. My office was just a short distance down the hallway from the courtroom, and the former judge followed closely behind on my heels. I invited him into my office.

Then he told me how he couldn't try the case that afternoon, how he had taken a previous dismissal and brought the case again, and so on. After listening to his complaints, I reminded him that his motion to continue the case had been denied and then said, "Now, be ready at two o'clock to start selection of the jury, or else report on the record that the case is settled." After great moans, groans, and howling, he left.

Since I was in the habit of leaving my door to my office open when various people came in to see me, my judicial assistant, Marilyn Ellis, had heard the entire conversation. Her desk was about five feet from my door. After the attorney left the chambers, I called to her, "Marilyn, I know how good you are with computers and such, can you make me a wall hanging of some kind?" Marilyn came into my office smiling and asked, "What kind of document are you thinking about?"

"I really want a commemoration or something that looks like all the rest of these fancy documents on this wall." On the wall next to the office door hung my two Wake Forest diplomas, my law license, and my certificates of admission to the United States Supreme Court, the Fourth Circuit, and also the United States District Court for the Eastern District of North Carolina. So, I began to describe to her what it was that I was thinking I wanted. I then went to lunch and returned in the afternoon to open court at two o'clock. The attorney and the defendant's lawyer reported the case as settled and it was subsequently dismissed.

That afternoon, having paid her usual close attention to my needs and desires, Marilyn presented to me a framed eight-and-a-half-by-eleven-inch wall hanging that looked a little like this:

THE STATE OF NORTH CAROLINA TO THE VARIOUS ATTORNEYS, ASSOCIATES, AND ATTENDANTS OF THIS COURT:

The undersigned Senior Resident Superior Court Judge of Judicial District 3A makes the following declaration:
KWITCHURBELYAKIN
Given at Greenville in the State of North Carolina
This 6th day of August, 2002

With my signature and a bright gold seal on the left of the document, it was official. Marilyn had done a beautiful job. We hung it on the wall beside the Fourth Circuit certificate, and there it rested for the next fourteen years. Several times over those following years, a young lawyer or some curious friend would come visit and gazing on all the diplomas and certifications, I would notice the eye of the examiner peering quizzically at the untypical and perplexing command, *KWITCHURBELYAKIN*. Earnestly applying the fixed principles of phonetics would eventually reveal its meaning.

TV and the Courtroom

When a camera, especially a video camera, is pointed in our direction, our minds change and we tend to focus, as does the camera, on our own actions. When the lens is pointed in our direction, we become the center of our thoughts and behavior. We either consciously or subconsciously begin to fashion and shape whatever is happening at the moment to our purposes and magnified image. In this situation, our obligation and responsibility to be aware of our present task may be diminished.

Before the addition of the annex and other improvements made to our Pitt County Courthouse in the 1990s, it was necessary that prisoners and defendants engaged in an ongoing trial be escorted by sheriff's deputies through a public area to the superior court courtroom. This public area was, of course, open to access by television camera crews. The prisoners and defendants would on occasion exhibit poor behavior. The prisoner may kick at the camera or shout a word or two in their obvious irritation at being restrained and having to be in the courthouse. The scene would give the viewer an impression that the courthouse was a place of disorder and sometimes chaos. When I became the senior resident judge, I approached the TV crewmen and presented them with an alternative.

This was before the televised O.J. Simpson murder trial. It was only on rare occasions that judges would invite TV cameras into the courtroom. My proposal to the TV camera crews was that I would allow them to film the courtroom proceedings on a limited basis if they would agree to forego the filming of the transport of prisoners and defendants inside the courthouse. I let them know that I could govern the degree and the distance from which they would be allowed to film the prisoner or defendant. I also shared with them that it was my observation that all they really wanted was some background film footage to show as they made their reports of the activities at the courthouse.

It was then established that one TV camera would be permitted to set up in a back corner of the courtroom for a limited time at the beginning of a trial. No juror's face would be allowed to be filmed, and upon my signal the camera would be removed. The camera would be allowed to film the proceedings on the first day of a trial until the eleven o'clock morning recess, and the TV stations would share the film footage with one another. After the morning recess the crew would be asked to remove their cameras from the courtroom.

Thereafter the crews became accustomed to leaving at the first day's morning recess without the direction from the court. On occasion the TV film crew would be allowed to film at the time of the jury returning a verdict. As the years went by, I occasionally allowed more than one camera crew to film. This procedure worked very well throughout the remainder of my time on the bench. The lawyers cooperated admirably. I did not concern myself with whether other judges using the Pitt County courtroom allowed the proceedings before their courts to be filmed. That was their sole choice and determination.

On the many occasions when I was called to preside over well-known and notable cases in other counties, I would have my bailiffs invite the TV crews into the courtroom. Their cameras would be situated in a back corner of the courtroom. Upon the first morning's eleven o'clock recess, I would instruct the bailiff to inform the camera crews that they were to leave the courtroom. The crews seemed to understand the instruction and would follow the court's direction without complaint. They had acquired their background footage.

Once, when I arrived in Goldsboro to preside over a murder trial, I found numerous TV station trucks with their extended antennas surrounding the courthouse. A courthouse addition and renovation project was under way and the case would be tried in a small temporary courtroom. The TV crews asked permission to film inside the courtroom, and I asked the bailiff to direct them to set up in a corner.

At ten o'clock the proceedings began with the hearing of some preliminary matters. The jury had been summoned to report that afternoon, and jury selection was scheduled to begin at two o'clock. As we proceeded through the matters to be heard that morning, I began to notice that one of the defendant's lawyers seemed to be "playing to the cameras." At the morning's eleven o'clock recess, I asked the bailiff to tell the TV crews that during the recess they were to remove their cameras from the courtroom, as was our practice in Pitt County.

When we returned to the courtroom from our morning recess, the defense lawyer asked if he could approach the bench. Upon his request I responded, "Yes, all the lawyers may approach the bench." The defendant's two lawyers came forward and were joined by the two lawyers for the state. One of the defense lawyers, with a quizzical glance, said, "Judge, why did you tell the TV cameras to leave?" I responded, "That's just the way I do things." He quickly responded, "Well Judge, I just don't understand that." I then said, "Well, let me explain it to you. You ain't no Errol Flynn and I ain't no Cecil B. DeMille." The defense lawyer said again, "Well Judge, I don't understand that at all." I then said, "You go on back over and sit down behind your table and think about it. It'll come to you." I think maybe the thought I intended to convey to him sunk in, as we did not have any further discussion on that subject.

A year or so after my bench conference with the Goldsboro lawyer, we all watched with derision the pitiful display of the shameful influence that TV cameras can have and their impact on justice in the courtroom. The nationwide telecast of the trial of O.J. Simpson graphically exhibited how a trial court could become overwhelmed by the presence of cameras. We witnessed our obligation and responsibility to be aware of our present task, our professional obligation and assignment, tragically and shamefully diminished. There may have been occasions when I allowed my conduct of a trial to be less than it ought to have been, but it was never because of a TV camera.

The Courthouse

A resident Superior Court Judge holds court on a weekly basis where assigned by the Chief Justice of the Supreme Court of North Carolina. The judge enjoys the sole function of holding court and hearing cases brought before him. The judge is a circuit-riding general-jurisdiction trial judge. On any given week civil and criminal cases appear on the docket in the county to which the judge is assigned by the Chief Justice. Without any other duties of an administrative nature, the Resident Judge hears the cases as they are called by the district attorney in the criminal courts and as the judge calls the cases on the civil docket.

After having been elected in 1990 as a resident Superior Court Judge, I filed for re-election. The law required that my judgeship be synced with the election of the Senior Resident Superior Court Judge. The senior resident and I, and any other person to file for election, would run for the two positions in November 1992, and the winners would be the two who received the highest number of votes.

Judge David Reid, the Senior Resident Superior Court Judge of Judicial District 3A, Pitt County, and I were the only two people to file in January 1992 for the two superior court positions and, being unopposed, we were elected for eight-year terms in the November 1992 election. Just after the election, though, came the sad news that our beloved senior resident judge was suffering with terminal cancer. Immediately, jockeying for the anticipated vacancy began.

The second Superior Court Judgeship, the resident judgeship, had been created by the North Carolina General Assembly just three years before with a specific candidate in mind. For whatever reason, however, the intended candidate had not run for election. With the impending death of the senior resident judge, that person became the anticipated appointee of the Democratic Governor-Elect, but another courthouse official was also interested in the position. Because the incumbent governor was a Republican, all these plans and visions hinged on the survival of the senior resident judge until the January 1993 inauguration of the new Democratic governor.

While a Republican governor resided quietly in the Governor's Mansion in Raleigh, our newly re-elected Senior Resident Superior Court Judge, David Reid, died on the last Monday of December 1992. By the end of the week the Republican governor would appoint a young aide to fill the position of Resident Superior Court Judge of Judicial District 3A, Pitt County. The hopes and dreams of the two Democrats who sought to fill the seat were dashed upon the hard rocks of time. The young aide, Mark Martin, would go on to serve admirably as a trial judge and as an appellate judge and eventually became the Chief Justice of the North Carolina Supreme Court, the highest judicial office in the State.

Upon the death of Judge Reid, his trial court coordinator telephoned me in West Virginia with the sad news. My family was enjoying an after-Christmas ski trip. The senior resident position had come to rest upon my shoulders. The various administrative duties assigned to the position were now mine, so instead of the relatively tranquil life of a regular trial judge whose only duty was to hear cases, my responsibilities now included the general care of the courthouse, the management of the civil docket, the appointment of magistrates and clerks, and the scheduling of civil and criminal terms of court.

PART III:
THE COURTROOM CREW

The Courthouse Redeemed

During my first week serving as the new Senior Resident Judge in January 1993, the trial court administrator proudly informed me that there was a plan to abandon our old Pitt County courthouse and convert it into a museum. He let me know that plans for a new courthouse had been approved by the county commissioners. The new courthouse building was to be located across the Tar River, north of the city of Greenville, on the county's rural administrative agency campus. I had never heard about these plans, but I was aware of a trend throughout the state where counties were abandoning their historic courthouses and erecting "modern" structures in their place. I suppose that I should have figured that the big vacant lot in the middle of the campus overlooking the new lake and surrounded by the new county buildings was meant for the new future courthouse.

I felt sad as I considered the sorry fate of the old Pitt County courthouse. My father was a county commissioner at the time, and so far as I can remember, had not mentioned to me the relocation of the Pitt County courthouse. No one, including our recently departed senior resident judge, had ever told me of the plans. The trial court administrator confidently assured me that the old courthouse building would survive the move to become a county museum. He was excited about the prospect and he knew of several counties across our state that had done this very thing and built fine new state-of-the-art courthouses. He reported with authority that those counties were well-pleased, and that I too ought to be pleased with Pitt County's plans. He asked if I would like to see the approved plans. I remained silent as the words, "I'll be dadgummed if this is going to happen," ran through my mind. I have still never laid eyes on those plans.

It has long been a tradition in my family to have a meal after church on Sundays at my parents' home in Farmville. On Sunday, January 9, 1993, our family enjoyed a typically delicious Sunday dinner following church. After lunch my father verified all that the trial court administrator had told me. He said that the plans for the new courthouse had been approved, but that there had been no requests for bids for the construction. He assured me that this intention to move the courthouse was an integral part of the county's long-range plan to have all the county buildings on the campus established for that purpose. My father was very surprised that I had known nothing of the plans, but no one had mentioned them to me. He could easily sense my disapproval of the idea.

My next step was to call the county architect. In our telephone conversation the following week, the architect verified everything my father and the trial court administrator had told me, including the firmness of the county's intent to follow the long-established plan to build the new courthouse on the county office campus. In the telephone conversation the county architect reluctantly agreed to meet with me on the first Saturday of February in 1993.

Our meeting began with the architect letting me know that he had been feeling a bit out of place since the county commission had made its decision. Upon being assured that as the Senior Resident Superior Court Judge for the county I had the authority to talk with him about the use of the courthouse, we began to talk about the old 1912 courthouse, the building in which we then sat.

I mentioned that I had held several terms of court in Wayne County, and that the original architect of the Wayne County courthouse was the same one who designed the Pitt County courthouse. Both courthouses were constructed early in the second decade of the twentieth century. Although the Pitt County courthouse is smaller, the two courthouses have the same floor plan. Having held several weeks of court in Wayne County while an annex to their courthouse was under construction, I was inspired by their plans and had a vision of the addition of a similar annex to the Pitt County courthouse.

Our county architect listened with interest as I told him how the people of Wayne County were saving their historic courthouse with the planned addition. We talked for at least two hours as I shared with him my vision for the Pitt County courthouse. My dream included an annex to be built in the back parking lot with an atrium between the annex and our historic courthouse. I described to the architect the re-bricking, a "new skin," for the 1968 annex attached to the west side. Finally, I shared with him my dream of the restoration of the old historic courtroom in our courthouse. At my suggestion, the architect and I walked off the footprint of the atrium and the new annex. I carefully explained the way that I envisioned the three buildings fitting together, and he seemed to be a little interested. With the dedicated help of many friends, almost ten years later to the day, I was able to see all three phases of the vision come to pass.

The next step was to get the county commissioners to listen. The old historic courthouse was leaking badly. Noticeable damage was being done by the rainwater and something needed to be done to save the building. The courthouse needed a new roof, and I knew that Sunday dinner at my father's table in Farmville would be coming soon enough.

Sunday afternoons after the family meal were usually spent visiting with my mother and father and the family. Sometime in March or April of 1993, my father invited me to go with him on a Sunday afternoon drive. He wanted to check on something at his Greene County farm, which was located four or five miles south of Farmville. It was a good way to spend Sunday afternoon. Upon arriving at the farm, we walked about outside the small house and around the curtilage. I praised how well the buildings and their roofs were maintained. My father, the county commissioner, responded: "Buddy (his term of endearment for me), the roof is a very important part of any building. If the roof is leaking, then the building won't last long."

Returning home to Farmville, I told my father about the leaking roof on our Pitt County courthouse. I knew that as a county commissioner, he would feel duty-bound to do all within his power to see that the buildings owned by the county were properly maintained. He said that he was unaware of the poor condition of the seventy-five-year-old copper roof and the water damage to the courthouse. He promised me that he would look into the situation the following day.

The majority of the county commission at that time was made up of members of the "Greatest Generation." Most of the members owned at least one farm with farm buildings. All of the commissioners knew the importance of having a good roof on the courthouse. A likeness of the courthouse building was in the middle of the seal of Pitt County, and the building had become a symbol of the county government. I knew that if the members of the commission invested in a new copper roof for the courthouse then it would be hard for them to abandon that fine old symbol of Pitt County. My hunch was correct. In 1994 a bright shiny new copper roof was put on the Pitt County courthouse.

By 2003, ten short years later, we, the people of Pitt County, had built the new annex on the exact footprint that the county architect and I had walked off on that February day in 1993. The annex, housing courtrooms and judges' chambers, was completed. A beautiful and spacious atrium now bridged the old courthouse and the new annex. Judge Clifton Everett, the other Superior Court Judge, named the atrium area "Courthouse Lane," as that space had originally been a small alley behind the courthouse. A new brick veneer was put on the 1968 annex. The old historic superior court courtroom was completely restored to its original graceful beauty.

A modern and spacious atrium now serves as the main public entrance to the courthouse, the new annex, and the 1968 annex. The new annex has five well-designed district court courtrooms, two superior court courtrooms, and five chambers for the District Court Judges. The Pitt County sheriff currently occupies the first floor of the 1968 annex and portions of the original building. The Register of Deeds has moved out of the original building, and the sheriff has moved into new quarters near the jail. The clerk of court now occupies three of the four floors of the 1968 annex. The old historic courtroom is the most magnificent temple of justice in the eastern part of our great state. The courthouse project has been a blessing for the people of Pitt County and a special blessing for downtown Greenville, our county seat. The historic Pitt County courthouse has been saved for future generations.

In a portion of my remarks upon the opening of Superior Courtroom #1 in 2003, I told the audience, "Saint Augustine said that the human mind was particularly delighted when truth was presented to it indirectly, like in symbols and sacred places. Courtrooms today are designed without any sense of the iconic because moderns like straightforward, unambiguous communication. We want factories and sterile scientific laboratories rather than majestic places that bring forth the spiritual nature of human beings.' This space (the historic Pitt County Courtroom), this Courtroom, I love!

"We did not focus on the utilitarian. We focused on the beauty of the justice and truth found here. The beauty of the procedure that begins with the judge saying, "Call your next case" and continues with the calling of a jury into the box, the lawyers' opening statements, the testimony, the closing arguments, the law, the verdict, the truth. Here we do the work of the people and the Lord. We seek justice defined in that center window behind me. We seek "to render to one his due."'

The Wonderful Jury

The most enjoyable aspect of my job as a judge was my interaction with the jury. The jury is the backbone of our judicial system, giving intrinsic authority and credibility to the administration of justice in our communities. In criminal cases the jury, applying the law of proof beyond a reasonable doubt, is the firewall protecting the people from the overzealous prosecutor.

I presided over many criminal trials, and in each of those trials I instructed the jury that they were to find the true facts of the case and render or return a verdict reflecting the truth as they found it to be. In the criminal case they were instructed that they were to find the facts beyond a reasonable doubt. Every verdict was returned by an act of faith. In every criminal, case the jury was not there when the criminal act took place. To return a verdict against the defendant in a criminal trial, the jury had to believe the evidence beyond a reasonable doubt. Hebrews 11:1 tells us,

"Faith is the assurance about what we do not see," that the very limits of our reason make faith a necessity.

Speaking of democracy, Sir Winston Churchill wrote, "At the bottom of all the tributes paid to democracy is the little man, walking into the little booth, with a little pencil, making a little cross on a little bit of paper – no amount of rhetoric or voluminous discussion can possibly diminish the overwhelming importance of the point." And, to paraphrase Mr. Churchill, at the bottom of the tributes paid to our great judicial system of justice is the little man and the little woman, walking into the little jury box, with a little pen, making a little cross or check mark on a little bit of paper called a verdict sheet – no amount of rhetoric or voluminous discussion can possibly diminish the overwhelming importance of the jury and its faith.

Each weekly term of court brings a new group of jurors to the courthouse. We call the summoned individual citizens a jury pool. The jury pool is made up of the qualified people of the community—regular common citizens. It usually consists of about fifty to a hundred citizens who are summoned by random selection to serve at their local county courthouse for a weekly term. From this pool juries of twelve are chosen to hear individual cases. It is one of our greatest blessings that we place in the hands of ordinary citizens the determination of guilt or innocence of those accused of serious crimes. Every citizen is much happier and safer armed with the knowledge that their life, liberty, or property cannot be taken by a government functionary.

After being selected to serve on a case the jury listens to the testimony of the witnesses and makes a judgment as to the credibility of each of the witnesses called by the state or plaintiff. The jury considers the admissible evidence; that is, the whole of the testimony of the witnesses governed by the rules of evidence enforced by the trial judge. The jury is called upon to apply their common sense to the facts as the jurors find them to be, apply the law as given to them by the judge, and determine the matter of guilt.

About seventy or eighty prospective jurors would be summoned to court each week to serve on jury panels to hear and adjudicate cases. Except in one instance where a juror chose to wear a garment with a profane sentence written across the front, all of my interactions with jurors were very pleasant. The jurors of every county in which I held court were always cordial, punctual, and ready, willing, and able to serve in their assigned role. The jurors would listen to the clerk's instructions, to my instructions, to the lawyers and to the witnesses. Within the boundaries of the rules that I gave to them the jurors found the facts of the cases and otherwise did what they thought was right in the cases before the court. It was always an honor and privilege to serve alongside of them in our mutual quest for the truth.

The only time that it was my duty to address and correct

the conduct of a juror occurred in Pitt County on a Monday morning at the beginning of a weekly criminal term of court. A young man entered the courtroom wearing a sweatshirt with the words clearly printed on the front, "DON'T ASK ME FOR S---." About the time that the shirt drew my attention, one of my bailiffs asked to approach the bench. He asked if I had noticed the shirt and I acknowledged that I had. I then asked the bailiff to quietly approach the young man, who was now seated in the section of the courtroom provided for summoned jurors. The bailiff was instructed to ask the man two questions. The first question would be, "Do you know how to read?" If that question was answered affirmatively, then the bailiff was to ask the man the second question, "Do you know what that is that is printed on the front of your shirt?" If the man wearing the shirt answered that question "yes," then the bailiff was instructed to ask the man to accompany him to the outside of the courtroom and place him in custody until I had an opportunity to address his conduct. Shortly, the man was escorted out of the courtroom.

About an hour later, the remaining jurors having been excused from the courtroom for the morning recess, the man was brought into the bar. It was determined that the man had been summoned to the court to serve for the week as a juror. He was asked about his conduct and expressed no misunderstanding of the words, an obscene and defiant declaration, appearing on the front of his shirt. The young man was over twenty-one years old. He expressed no regret for wearing the garment into the courtroom. He seemed a bit incredulous that I would take notice of his shirt and question its use. The man was found to be in contempt of the court for wearing the garment inside the courtroom. It was ordered that he be confined in the county jail for a term of forty-eight hours. The jailer was ordered to burn the shirt after it had been photographed for inclusion in the criminal contempt file.

Because I had failed to state on the record that the court had "found beyond a reasonable doubt" that the young man was wearing the obscene shirt in my presence, the appellate court reversed his contempt conviction. A complaint was made by the ACLU to the Judicial Standards Commission, and no action was taken. Several reports and comments were made by newspapers. I recognize that thoughtless and inconsiderate people have the privilege to cheapen and demean the public square. The shameful obscenities now beheld by adults and children in the public places egregiously coarsens our culture. We citizens may have to tolerate the filth spewed forth by the callous and indifferent at the mall, but not in the courtroom.

There is no freedom of speech in the courtroom. Neither lawyers nor anyone else, including the trial judge, are allowed to intentionally embarrass or abuse people in the courtroom. People are prohibited from saying insulting things to the judge or any other court personnel. Those people who are in the courtroom are not allowed to treat lawyers, witnesses, or litigants with contempt. People in the courtroom must abide by the rules of the court. It takes a certain amount of decorum to maintain a place where one can be assured that their grievance can be heard.

Before administering the juror's oath to the summoned jurors, the courtroom clerk would address the entire pool and ask them if any of them would like to be excused from serving on the jury that week. Citing various reasons, some of the jurors would ask to be excused from having to serve. One of the excuses available is dismissal by the judge on account of age. In North Carolina a citizen over the age of seventy may be excused if the prospective juror wishes.

While I was presiding in Pitt County one week, a woman asked to approach the bench to whisper to me her request to be excused. At the judge's bench she said, "Judge, I would like to be excused from jury service this week." I replied, "Ma'am, why do you want to be excused?" She then hesitantly replied, "Judge, I'm seventy-five years old." To that I replied with a smile, "Well, Ma'am, you don't look a day older than fifty-five to me." She smiled broadly and said, "Thank you, Judge." She turned around and returned to be with the jury and served the remainder of the week. She served as a juror on two cases, and on one of those two cases she served as the foreman of the jury.

On two cases I had husbands and wives called forward

to sit on the same jury. Jurors are called to the jury box at random, and in one of those instances the husband and the wife sat side by side in seats seven and eight. The lawyers are allowed to question the jurors to determine whether the particular juror is a "good juror" for their case. When the lawyer for the defendant came to the husband he said, "Sir, a juror is required to listen to the evidence presented in the trial, make up his own mind about it and deliberate with the other jurors to reach a verdict. Do you think that you can do this?" The husband juror answered that he was able to do that. Then the lawyer said, "Now, suppose that what you think about the evidence is not the same as what your wife thinks. Do you think that you can hold to your opinion, if it's strongly held, and possibly find contrary to your wife?" Although everyone seemed to be incredulous, the husband replied, "Why yes, of course." Both were seated as jurors.

On occasion I would be called by friends seeking excusal from jury service. I would always tell them that I could not excuse them from jury duty. I would politely call their attention to the set procedure to seek excusal contained in their summons and urge them to take that course. In obvious disappointment, these friends would politely say thank you and hang up. I had a friend in my Sunday School class call me and we went through this very conversation. She then dutifully reported to court to serve. On the first case called for trial, her name, called at random, was broadcast by the courtroom clerk. My friend, who is a feisty, independent woman, stood and walked toward the bar, and on her way she made a face at me as she took her place in seat number one in the jury box. Since she was facing me with the audience at her back, the courtroom clerk noticed my friend's nasty look and apparently no one else did. My friend served on the jury and, until this day, is convinced that I rigged the deal and had the clerk call her name. I promise that I did not.

On a Thursday afternoon of a week of a criminal court term in Hertford County, we picked and empaneled a jury in a misdemeanor case that we intended to try the next day. At the end of each week of a jury session, most often on a Thursday afternoon after selecting a jury, I would dismiss the selected and empaneled jury with instructions to return the next morning. Before dismissing the remaining jurors, I would take a few minutes to give them an opportunity to ask any questions about anything that they may have observed during the week of court. I would thank them all and tell them that the jury is the very backbone of our judicial system. I would remind them that the jury was the most reliable and true fact finder and that should one word be exhibited on a marquee for the courthouse, it would be the word "Truth."

I restated the parting words of my jury instructions to them in each case that they had heard that week: "That you are to find the true facts of the case and render a verdict reflecting the truth as you find it." I would tell them that, as members of the community, their verdicts carried the authority of the people and that their decisions had the respect of the community. I would then remind the jurors that as citizens they were the sovereign under our miraculous Constitution that begins with the words, "We the people." I would finally remind them of the words of President John Adams, that as long as the people of this country are good, the nation will be great. I would then send them on their way with the assurance that they would not be summoned for jury service again for at least two years.

It would take me a little over an hour to drive home from Winton in Hertford County, and then I would return the next morning to finish the week. When I arrived at the courthouse, I was informed that the defendant in the case we were to try had changed his mind and had decided to enter a plea of guilty. The jury was in the jury box in the center of the room waiting to hear the case, and they watched as the defendant pled guilty. I noticed that there were other lawyers in the courtroom and one in particular had a client charged with impaired driving who wanted a jury trial. So, I called the lawyer and prosecutor to the bench and I asked them if they would find the jury in the box satisfactory to hear the impaired driving case. After the prosecutor consulted his officer and the defense lawyer consulted his client, the jury was empaneled to hear the impaired driving case and we finished that case about mid-afternoon and I went home to Greenville. Nice week.

My Bailiffs

While at a morning recess in Pitt County a number of lawyers had gathered in an anteroom between the courtroom and the judge's chambers. The room was fairly crowded and most of its occupants were standing. A coffee machine was on a wooden countertop that was made of the same wood and stained the same color as the fine oak paneling in the room. My bailiff came up to me and asked, "Judge, do you want me to bring you a cup of coffee? I replied very gratefully, "Yes, that would be very nice." In just a few seconds the bailiff presented me with a Styrofoam cup and said, "Here's your coffee, Judge."

I took the cup from my bailiff and looked at it and said, "Donald, what do you see in this cup?" He responded questioningly as he peered down into the cup, "I don't know, Judge. Is it grounds?" I then said, "No, I don't see any grounds. What do you think you see, Donald?" He hesitantly responded, "I don't see anything, Judge." Then I smiled and said, "Yes, you do, Donald. You see the bottom." After that day he always brewed strong, perfectly tasting coffee, dark enough that the bottom of the cup could not be seen until the last drop was consumed.

On another occasion, we had been involved for about three days in a very intense trial in Wayne County of a defendant charged with assault with a deadly weapon with intent to kill, inflicting serious injury. The defendant was from a very contrary and clannish rural family, and there had been a shootout in his front yard. A deputy sheriff, who had been married for about two weeks, had been wounded and was paralyzed from the waist down. The state had presented its case and now the defendant's lawyer was presenting the evidence for the defendant.

The Wayne County Courthouse was undergoing renovation, and a large annex was being added to the original building. We were in a small, crowded, and uncomfortable temporary courtroom. The case was somewhat emotional and closely watched by law enforcement and the public. Every day the high sheriff of the county would sit for an hour or two in the courtroom intently observing the proceedings. The bailiff, Mr. Harvell, carefully and conscientiously watched every movement in the courtroom. The family felt that they had been severely abused by the sheriff of the county. The defendant displayed very little remorse. You could feel the tension in the air, and Mr. Harvell had reminded me that the courthouse did not have the means to screen everyone who entered the building.

Presently, the lawyer for the defendant called the defendant's father to the witness stand. The large, rough-looking, country man came up, raised his right hand, and swore to tell the whole truth. The father told the story as he was satisfied and certain that it was, free from any doubt that the entire sorry shootout sprung from the failing and shortcoming of law enforcement officers. He protested that the sheriff's deputies had provoked the roughness and ferocity of the battle. His testimony did nothing to help his son's chances of going home a free man. As he testified, the disturbed and agitated father sat in the witness chair no more than an arm's length from me. After a crushing cross-examination by the district attorney, the disconcerted and befuddled father stepped down from the witness chair and returned to the front row bench of the audience.

Mr. Harvell very calmly and patiently asked permission to approach the judge's bench. He came forward and softly and under his breath asked me to take a recess. Although it was not the time for a recess. I immediately asked the jury to follow a bailiff to the jury room and then announced with a very clear voice, "The court will be at recess for fifteen minutes." I rose from the bench, and an armed deputy followed me to the judge's chambers behind the courtroom. He informed me that Mr. Harvell had heard a "clump" on the bench when the defendant's father had sat down on the courtroom pew. I then heard some raised voices in the courtroom and what sounded like some brief tussling.

When I returned to the courtroom the father of the defendant was standing before me in handcuffs. Mr. Harvell then reported to me that he had taken a small .38 revolver from the old irascible man. The gun had been tucked in his back trousers pocket. We had a short hearing, and the father was found in contempt of court for violating the posted prohibition of possessing a firearm in the courtroom. The father was sentenced to thirty days in the Wayne County jail, the jury was returned to the courtroom without an inkling of what had happened, and the trial continued peacefully. A good and very experienced bailiff had followed his keen instincts and possibly saved the day. Mr. Harvell was a great man.

After the renovations and additions to the Wayne County Courthouse were completed, the courts enjoyed some very nice facilities. The new courtrooms in the annex were large, spacious, and finely appointed. The original historic courtroom was completely restored, with the meticulously researched original paint colors placed back on the walls. The walls were painted in colors representing the color of tobacco in its various stages of the curing process. Shortly after the courthouse construction and renovation was completed, we tried a non-capital murder case in one of the new courtrooms. The defendant was a tough man who had spent most of his young life on the streets of the roughest neighborhoods of Goldsboro.

After almost a week trying the case, the jury indicated that they had reached their verdicts to the charges of murder and other very serious felonies. While the jury returned to the courtroom to announce their verdicts, the defendant took on an air of anxiousness and appeared to be disturbed and agitated. To avoid potential prejudice, it is the practice of the courts to refrain from the cuffing of defendants during their trials before a jury.

The defendant remained standing with his arms by his side as the jury filed into the courtroom. The bailiff stood directly behind the defendant. The jury's verdicts, finding the defendant guilty of all charges, were announced. Upon the announcement of the verdicts, the bailiff standing behind the defendant gently tapped the center of the lower back of the defendant. The defendant instinctively recognized the bailiff's expectation and put his hands behind his back, and the defendant was quietly cuffed. An experienced bailiff had grasped the distress and troubled spirit of the defendant. The bailiff reacted with a gentle measured approach that stilled the defendant's anxiety and his frightened apprehension of the years of confinement he faced.

Experts

Science seems to be the holy way, the truth, and the life of our brave new world, and the progressive man is its most dedicated adherent. This ancient materialistic religion follows the creed of the scientific method more fervently than the Christian man follows the Nicene Creed. Experts in the hard sciences like medicine, chemistry, biology, physics, and astronomy are its high priests. These scientific priests are usually ordained by universities and may be invested as doctors of this or that with strings of letters such as MD, JD, or PhD strung behind their surnames signifying their high and exalted offices. Along with their titles come the power and glory of expertise. Expertise is the assumption of status, much like holiness is to the Christian priest, rector, or pastor. The word of an expert is to be regarded as the ultimate authority. Common sense is blasphemy to the experts and is the stuff of nonsense or, worse, myth.

In the courtroom, this scientism is checked by the law of the land applied to specific facts. The word or opinion of the expert is considered by the common juror charged with the responsibility of finding the true facts of a case. Experts may appear in the courtroom as an accident reconstructionist, a medical doctor, an attorney, an engineer or even a grocery shelf stocker. The plaintiff comes into court with his experts, and the defendant comes into court with his. The experts for both sides are sure that the opinion that they hold is in fact the last word, that by all rights should hold sway on the question at hand.

The medical malpractice case is the most frequent and well-known civil action that brings forth the expert. In a medical malpractice case, the plaintiff alleges that he has been grievously injured by a medical doctor who failed to follow the standard of care in his treatment of the plaintiff's ailment or affliction. In the medical profession, a person with the "MD" attached to his surname is of the highest order of the priestly science business. When it comes to their particular medical specialty, few are recognized to have the status or knowledge to challenge their medical opinion. The courtroom is the forum where the certainty of expert opinion comes to meet the common sense of the common man seated as a common jury.

The jury is instructed that they are to consider the opinion of an expert witness, but they are not bound by it.

Then the jurors are reminded that they are not required to accept an opinion of an expert to the exclusion of facts and circumstances disclosed by other testimony. In other words, facts and circumstances matter. Reason matters. Common sense matters. Jurors are told that they "are the sole judges of the credibility of each witness and the weight to be given to the testimony of each witness." The people, sitting as the jury, make the determination as to whether the opinion of the expert makes any sense, whether it is credible under the circumstances.

As a young inexperienced trial judge, having been on the bench eleven months, I found myself presiding over a wrongful death case with five very experienced trial attorneys. Representing the plaintiff was the then-president of the North Carolina Bar Association and a young associate. A recognized trial attorney from Rocky Mount was on the plaintiff's side assisting. On the defendant's team was the vice president of the bar association along with the then-president of the North Carolina State Bar. I was surrounded by high-powered, very experienced trial lawyers.

The case arose out of an automobile collision that occurred on one morning in December three years earlier in which the plaintiff's son was killed. The plaintiff contended that the defendant was driving negligently and at a high rate of speed. The defendant denied that he was driving negligently and argued that the plaintiff was negligent and, even if the defendant was negligent, the plaintiff had the last clear chance to avoid the collision. To prove their claims, the plaintiff and the defendant both called two well-known experts in accident reconstruction to give their opinions as to what had happened.

The plaintiff's expert's opinion was that the defendant drove negligently and the defendant's expert had a firm opinion that the plaintiff was driving negligently. The plaintiff's expert testified that, in his opinion, the defendant was traveling at least eighty-one miles per hour prior to braking and that, at the point where the two automobiles came together, the defendant's vehicle was travelling at fifty-seven to sixty miles an hour. The defendant's expert testified that, in his opinion, the defendant was traveling within the fifty-five mile per hour speed limit, at a maximum speed of 54.7 miles per hour, prior to braking. The widely divergent opinions surprised no one, except possibly the jurors.

Our jurors find themselves called upon to consider the opinion of the experts, weigh their credibility, and, applying their common sense, make their findings and conclusions as to what happened. The fulfillment of this seemingly impossible task demonstrates and confirms the miraculous splendor of the jury trial. It is a thing worth seeing. And it was my privilege and delight, as a trial judge, to behold the work of the jury day in and day out.

Working with Lawyers

In the weekly session designated as criminal court it was the prerogative of the district attorneys to call the cases from a court calendar prepared by their office. All of the cases on the calendar would presumably be ready for trial or for some other disposition, such as a plea of guilty or a dismissal of the case by the district attorney. After the roll call of the defendants to determine their presence in the courtroom, the judge would simply address the prosecutor and say, "Call your first case." After the day was started in that fashion and that particular case was handled, it was, "Call your next case."

And so it carried on; we called this undertaking the "proceedings." When the district attorney was prepared and the lawyers were present and prepared, it was an exhilarating experience to see the court's business attended to with as much order and efficiency as the law and its procedures would allow. Lawyers are expected to know their cases and the law of the case and conduct themselves in a professional manner. In a civil session of court, the calendar was previously prepared by a trial court administrator or coordinator under the supervision of the Senior Resident Superior Court Judge. Like in the criminal sessions, all the cases on the calendar were presumably ready to be tried. It was the duty of the trial judge to call the cases for trial. The plaintiff, the defendant, and their lawyers would be present and expected to be prepared for the trial of the case.

It goes without saying that trial lawyers possess varying degrees of skill. Their reputation does precede them. The best lawyers are very knowledgeable and truly trustworthy, and they know and happily abide by the rules of courtroom decorum. These lawyers know their case and the law that applies and, having fully prepared, come into the courtroom with confidence. Because of this, a judge can accept with confidence what they maintain the facts of their case to be. These lawyers will not misstate the law and lead the court into error. Even when the judge rules incorrectly, the best lawyers gracefully accept the unfavorable ruling of the court and studiously avoid any detrimental remarks about the judge or his rulings.

Observing the best lawyers ply their trade was a great pleasure. These lawyers would confidently place their case in the hands of the judge, and sometimes the jury, with masterful precision. On one occasion I presided over a medical malpractice case where the doctor was alleged to have operated on the wrong vertebra of the patient's spine. Both the patient's lawyer and the defense lawyer possessed good reputations as trial lawyers. Throughout the trial neither lawyer objected to any of the evidence presented by the other side, except in one instance.

The evidence showed that the doctor had violated the standard of care, and immediately after the operation had admitted his mistake to the plaintiff and her husband and told them that he was very sorry for making the mistake by operating on the wrong vertebra. They both accepted his apology, forgave the doctor, and consented to a second operation.

The plaintiff's lawyer introduced evidence of the doctor's admission of negligence and strenuously objected to the admission of evidence offered by the defendant doctor's lawyer that the plaintiff had forgiven the neglect and had accepted the second operation by the defendant doctor. I ruled that the evidence of the admission opened the door to the evidence of the plaintiff's forgiveness. The plaintiff's lawyer gracefully accepted the ruling. The jury found no negligence on the part of the doctor. In that trial I was impressed at how prepared and knowledgeable the two lawyers were about medical procedures and the methods employed by neurosurgeons.

For most of the years of my service as a judge, the district attorney's office of Pitt County had several very good trial lawyers who were always prepared and who presented their cases in a fair and considered manner. One of those lawyers, who had a folksy familiar approach, was also particularly effective in his closing remarks to the jury. In one of his cases, I was extremely skeptical that he would obtain a conviction. I remember thinking that I probably should have granted the defendant's motion to dismiss the case. As this prosecutor began his closing statement to the jury, I listened intently as he laid out one item of incriminating evidence after another. I gradually began to realize that he would win his case and the jury would return a verdict of guilty, which they did. Final arguments, or closing statements, are arguably the most important aspect of a trial.

A lawyer can ask too many questions, amazing himself with his ability to get the sought-for answers from witnesses who seem to be helping the client win an acquittal. In one case the defendant was charged with the very onerous felony of assault with a deadly weapon with the intent to kill inflicting serious injury. It is a Class C felony so the defendant, if convicted, would be facing a lengthy prison sentence. The victim was a man who was attending a cookout in a vacant lot along N.C. 258 in the town of Fountain. At the trial the victim of the assault testified that the defendant shot him in the side of his neck and the bullet traveled through his neck and lodged in his left shoulder. The defendant's lawyer thoroughly questioned the victim on cross-examination. After being unable to shake the victim, the interrogation went something as follows:

Defendant's attorney: "Now, you had been at the picnic or barbeque all day, hadn't you?"

Victim: "Yes, I had been at the barbeque all day."

Defendant's attorney: "And, you had been drinking alcohol, beer and other alcoholic beverages, all day, hadn't you?"

Victim: "Yes, I had been drinking alcohol, beer and other alcoholic beverages all day."

Defendant's attorney: "You were very drunk, weren't you?"

Victim: "Yes, I was very drunk."

Defendant's attorney: "You get obnoxious when you've been drinking, don't you?"

Victim: "Yes, I get obnoxious when I've been drinking."

Defendant's attorney: "You curse and swear and just hang around when people want you to leave, don't you?"

Victim: "Yes, I curse and swear and just hang around when people want me to leave."

Defendant's attorney: "You cursed the defendant, didn't you?"

Victim: "Yes, I cursed the defendant."

It had become obvious that the victim was repeating almost verbatim the lawyer's questions. He had cooperated and confirmed everything that the lawyer thought he needed for the witness to avow. It looked like the defense lawyer was making headway. Then something like the following came forth.

Defendant's attorney: "You were just being a real jerk, weren't you?"

Victim: "Yes, I was being a real jerk, BUT.."

At this point the victim turned a little to his right toward my direction and the jury, in anticipation, leaned forward in their seats. Then the victim added: "You know, if you shot all the jerks in the world, there wouldn't be nobody left." And looking straight at me, plaintively asked, "Would there, Judge?"

Everybody in the courtroom but the defendant and his lawyer had just seen the defendant's goose cooked to well-done. The lawyer had asked too many questions. The defendant was found guilty as charged and, with his prior record leaning against him, received a lengthy prison sentence.

Each week of either civil and criminal court, approximately seventy to eighty citizens were summoned to serve as jurors. It made me very comfortable to keep the jury pool on the right-hand side in the courtroom while the district attorney was calling the cases. These potential jurors were able to watch the proceedings and observe the goings on in their local courthouse. The jury pool was always very interested, and the majestic Pitt County Superior Courtroom #1 was a very pleasant place to be. It was quiet enough for the jury pool to hear, and they could recognize friends who were lawyers and occasionally recognize a defendant or two.

On this particular day a spirited young assistant prosecutor was calling the cases. One defendant, pursuant to a plea bargain, entered a plea of guilty to simple possession of a controlled substance. The charge had been reduced from an original charge of possession of a controlled substance with the intent to sell and deliver it. The defendant happened to be from the west side of Greenville, and the controlled substance was cocaine. After taking the defendant's guilty plea and going over the plea bargain and hearing the defendant's lawyer, it was the prosecutor's time to address the court. From his substantial experience in my court, he knew exactly the judgment the court would enter in cases of this nature.

For probably five minutes the prosecutor went on and on with his remarks, purportedly addressed to the court. The recurring theme of his remarks was that the court needed to "send a message to the community," that the defendant's conduct would not go unnoticed nor unpunished, and that cocaine was a scourge on our city. I listened patiently and was amused that he clearly noticed that a good number of the jurors had figured out that this young prosecutor meant to send his message to them. He was obviously very pleased with himself.

I then turned to the defendant and there, sitting against the bar near the defendant's table, was an older man. Although very few fathers bother to appear with their sons in court, it occurred to me that maybe this distinguished looking man in work clothes was the defendant's father. I asked him to stand and I said, "Sir, do you have any interest in this case?" He replied in a strong voice that could be heard across the courtroom, "Yes sir, I am this young man's father." Then he added, "And if that young fellow over there (plainly referring to the young prosecutor) thinks that there is enough money in West Greenville to support the cocaine trade, then I don't know where he's living." I smiled and replied, "I know where he's living." The father then said, "You do, Judge? Where?" I then said, "He's living in LaLa Land." The father replied, "Yep, he sure is, Judge." At the recess the young prosecutor asked me why I would abuse him so harshly. I told him that he went out of his league when he waxed so eloquently before the jury and that his remarks were properly to be addressed to me. He graciously acknowledged his error and promised to do better in the future.

Some lawyers, like most people, I would guess, prefer that all their obligations be subservient to their own schedule. This sort has a propensity to ignore the boundaries set by the rules of life and the rules of court. Their motto seems to be, "Such rules and the behavior they engender be damned; I'm going to do what I want to do." I was holding a two-week session of criminal court in Craven County in the late nineties. The session had gone well and we had tried some cases and taken several pleas. On Wednesday of the second week, the prosecutor stood and announced that all of the cases on the docket had been addressed. The prosecutor requested that the clerk give the jurors that message when they were to call in that afternoon to get instructions as to when to report back to court.

Out in the courtroom were seated eight young men who appeared to be awaiting the call of their case. I asked the prosecutor who these people might be, and he responded that he did not know. Again, he assured me that the calendar was complete and that all of the docket was done. No lawyers were present. The only people in the courtroom with me were the clerk, the prosecutor, the court reporter, and two bailiffs. I called the eight young men up to the inside of the bar and began to ask each his name. As each of them responded, the prosecutor flipped through the pages of his docket and announced either that the man's case had been dismissed or continued, except for the last two. These men had sat in the courtroom for almost two weeks without being informed by their lawyer or the prosecutor of the status of their cases.

When I asked the seventh man his name, the prosecutor responded with the name of his lawyer and added that the case was still open. The man, who was charged with driving while impaired, then took the next minute or two to tell me that he had been in court for the past week-and-a-half, that he had not seen his lawyer in the courtroom or anywhere else, that he had tried to contact his lawyer, and that he could not afford to continue to come to court with nothing being done about his case. He was agitated. Naming the same lawyer, the eighth man sang the exact same song, just the second verse. I then asked the clerk to telephone Lawyer So-and-So's office, which I thought was there in New Bern near the courthouse. He had been in New Bern for more than twenty-five years. The clerk informed me that Lawyer So-and-So had moved to Pitt County and that his office was now in Greenville, about forty-five miles away.

I considered the situation and determined our course of action. I told the clerk to leave an afternoon message for the jury pool to call back the next morning at eleven o'clock for further instructions and a possible return to the court at two o'clock. Both men's cases would require a jury, should either of them request a trial. I then told the clerk to call their lawyer's Greenville office and inform him that he was to appear the following morning at nine o'clock. The clerk returned to the courtroom and reported that she had talked with a woman who said she was Lawyer So-

and-So's secretary and that she would relay the message to the lawyer. I left the courtroom in the mid-afternoon and enjoyed a leisurely drive to my home in Greenville.

When we opened court in New Bern the next morning at nine o'clock there was no Lawyer So-and-So, but his clients were there waiting when I entered the courtroom. "Well," I said, "maybe Mr. Lawyer So-and-So didn't understand that we were going to open court at nine o'clock, and we'll wait until nine-thirty." At nine-thirty there was no Lawyer So-and-So. Then I called the bailiff forward and told him to have the lawyer standing in front of me within the hour. The bailiff, grinning like a mule eating briars, said that it would be done.

My impression was that he had known this lawyer and observed his ways for many years, and that finally there was going to be some accountability. At ten-thirty I entered the courtroom and the clerk reported that the local sheriff, with the assistance of the Pitt County Sheriff's office, had escorted Lawyer So-and-So to New Bern from his office in Greenville. She informed me that the lawyer was upset but, with the agreement of the prosecutor, had remanded his cases back to the district court from which the cases had been appealed. She then told me that he didn't have a way back to Greenville. I had known the lawyer for years and told her to tell him that I would give him a ride back to Greenville. Court was adjourned.

The courtroom clerk came back to my chambers while I was packing my computer and robe to leave and told me that Lawyer So-and-So declined my offer to give him a lift to Greenville. The next thing that I heard of Lawyer So-and-So was that he had filed to run against me in the election of 2000. During the campaign it was reported that the lawyer, soon to be an unsuccessful candidate for Superior Court Judge, complained that I was just not very nice. As a judge it was my intent to hold lawyers' feet to the fire in a respectful manner with a graceful and patient spirit.

During my more than twenty-five years serving as a judge in our courts interacting and working with hundreds of lawyers, I had occasion to find three lawyers in contempt. Although I can think of no reason why I did not find Lawyer So-and-So in contempt for delaying the court, I did find another lawyer in contempt for being late and hindering the work of the court. I did so primarily because he caused a seated jury to wait for him for forty-five minutes and upon his arrival to court offered no excuse or apology to the court or to the jury for his conduct. I sentenced the lawyer to seventy-two hours in the Northampton County jail. After serving twenty-four hours and upon his request to return to court and apologize in open court, I reduced his fine and his seventy-two-hour sentence to twenty-four hours confinement or time served.

Prosecutors

My experience has taught me that the best way to get a district attorney to take care of his docket is to put a jury in the courtroom. Although I have not had the experience of prosecuting cases, and so I could not, with any acuity, ascertain their thoughts, it has been my keen impression that some in that formidable and menacing office look upon the judge as a mere obstacle in their holy pursuit of the unrighteous malefactors bedeviling our communities. It seems that from the point of view of the prosecutor, the defendant most certainly ought to plead guilty as charged. In a small percentage of cases, that is not what happens. The defendant wants his trial by jury. From his citadel the prosecutor exclaims, "What? Plead 'Not guilty?'" Those two words, 'Not guilty,' call forth a contest, a court case, an examination of the evidence, before a judge and a jury of twelve tried-and-true citizens.

The rules provide that when a judge sustains an objection

to a question posed to the witness, ruling that the evidence called for by the question is inadmissible, that question cannot be again asked of the witness. On two occasions, in two different courts, separated by many years, prosecutors asked the witness an identical question after I had sustained an objection.

Both instances involved prosecutors who were very aggressive and who passionately believed that they were about the Lord's work. The first instance occurred in the early 1990s. When the prosecutor asked the question the second time, the defendant's lawyer jumped up and exclaimed, "Objection, Your Honor, that's the very same question that the court just sustained my objection to!" After the defense lawyer's objection, I called the prosecutor and the defendant's lawyer to the bench.

I looked at the prosecutor for a few seconds and then said, "Mr. So-and-So, do you remember that last case where you talked so badly about the defendant, that fellow in the plea hearing a few minutes ago that I sentenced to thirty years?" The prosecutor replied, "Yes Judge, what's that case got to do with this case?" I then replied, "I'll tell you what it's got to do with this case. If you ever again ask a witness the identical question that's been sustained, I'm going to put you in the same cell with him." The prosecutor was very apologetic and never again committed that grievous wrong.

On the second occasion that I sustained an objection to

a question previously asked of a witness, I was in the courtroom with a young assistant district attorney who was full of vim and vigor. He proudly considered that his youthful energy and zest aimed at prosecuting the defendant was a thing to be admired. In his eagerness to ensure that "right" prevailed, he seemed to sometimes forget himself and break the bounds of professional conduct. Because of this young fellow's stiff-necked response to instruction in the past, I came down hard on him in the presence of the jury and everyone in the courtroom after he asked a question that had been previously sustained.

Knowing the assistant prosecutor's boss and his probable reaction to my harsh public rebuke of his assistant, I had the court reporter type a transcript of the questions the assistant had asked. When court had ended for the day and I was in my chambers, the district attorney came into my office, sat down, and said, "Judge, why were you so hard on my man?" I greeted my friend with a smile, handed him the court reporter's transcript, and asked, "Well, tell me how you would have handled it." He read the transcript and shook his head. We had a pleasant conversation about other matters and he left my office.

The next day the assistant came up to me in the hallway and tried to apologize for his conduct. I ask him where the offense for which he offered an apology had occurred. He said, "Well Judge, it happened in the courtroom." I replied,

"Yes, and that is where an appropriate apology ought to be offered." He later apologized in the courtroom, and I readily accepted his apology. I regret, however, that the jury before whom he had failed to follow the rules was no longer present.

Not long into my two-year tenure as a District Court Judge, I had occasion to be the judge in a criminal case involving a sensitive family situation that I cannot fully recall. In the course of prosecuting the case, the female prosecutor began to shed tears and become emotional. I called the young prosecutor and the defense lawyer to the bench. I looked at her very sternly and asked her, "Do you have a law license?" To this question she quickly became of sober mind and responded, "Yes, sir, of course I do." I then said to her, "Then you need to dry your tears. You gave up your right to cry in the courtroom when you accepted your law license." She stopped crying, and over the years she became a better prosecutor.

The Expectation of Professionalism

It is my considered opinion that being a lawyer is a very high calling, perhaps the highest calling. The role of lawyers in the maintenance of civil order in our communities and our country cannot be fully appreciated without a close observance of their daily work. Lawyers guide and counsel their clients in the necessary complexities and complications of the law and its administration. The lawyer is knowledgeable of the law and the procedures necessary to apply it to the circumstances in which people sometime find themselves.

My interaction with lawyers, inside and outside the courtroom, has given me a healthy respect for the ones who are prepared and capable of performing their professional duties to their client without becoming emotionally entangled in the rulings of the court and the outcome of the case. As I share my court stories it is imperative that the reader constantly keep in mind that all of the stories are taken out of context. Not one of these stories that took place in a courtroom is an isolated occurrence. There is always more going on than meets the eye.

Not long ago a young lawyer told a "Judge Duke Story" in my presence. Several friends were listening intently and enjoying the lawyer's ability to spin a good yarn. Using a low voice at appropriate times to describe the manner I addressed him, he described how, upon his entering the courtroom and coming down the center aisle, I said, "What time do you have, Mr. Lawyer?" Mr. Lawyer stopped walking and responded with a relaxed voice, "It's 2:02, Judge." Then he told how, in a low voice with my eyes intently leveled at his, I said, "Court started back this afternoon at 2 o'clock." He ended his story with the observation that he was never again late for my court.

Now, that sounds pretty tough. It probably wasn't. Taking the story with everything that was going on, Mr. Lawyer was, more than likely, expected for a hearing or even engaged in an ongoing trial. In those circumstances Mr. Lawyer should have been seated behind the defense table ready to go to work when I entered the courtroom at 2 o'clock. Over the years I have had several young lawyers come up to me and thank me for "making them better lawyers." In various ways they have told me that once they had successfully tried a case in front of Judge Duke, then they had plenty of confidence to try cases in front of any judge.

It was my task to "teach" young lawyers that it was their duty to be a true professional. It was understood that my idea of a true professional was a lawyer who followed the rules, was on time, and was prepared to try the case. And several have shared with me that they knew that that was what I expected. They have told me that I showed no favoritism, and if a lawyer did not measure up to those three expectations of mine then the lawyer could expect no "kid glove" treatment. I did not have occasion to raise my voice. Some judges, who had the same expectations, were inclined to whisper their disappointment and corrections at the bench or in chambers. I did not, opting to voice my instructions out loud in the courtroom.

All lawyers and judges have heard judges say, "Court will start when I get there." This is usually taken to mean that the judge has no qualms about opening court later than the time scheduled for it to begin. I have always cringed when I have heard a judge say such a thing. It undoubtedly reveals either a greatly swollen spirit of hubris and pomposity or a greatly abbreviated awareness of the respect that is due jurors, litigants, clerks, bailiffs, and lawyers. The tone of condescension is palpable.

Although I have always had a great respect for lawyers and acknowledged and appreciated their considerable contribution to the peace of our communities, I have not held to the notion that a judge should quietly accommodate laziness and unprofessional conduct. Like judges, lawyers should be held to the rules. Generally speaking, plaintiffs' lawyers seem to expect more accommodation for their wants and desires, taking on an attitude of self-righteousness. They seem to expect that all others should recognize the virtue of their undertaking, their case that oftentimes becomes a cause. In civil cases plaintiffs' lawyers, more than defense lawyers, seem to expect judges to bend or expand the law to further their cases.

Plaintiffs' lawyers, maybe because of the outsized investment they have in the case, the "righteousness" of their cause, or the fact that they will be paid only if they win, seem inordinately intent on just winning. It is my firm belief that a courtroom is a place where objective truth and justice are to be sought. By adhering closely to the rules of trial procedure and to the rules of evidence, the quest for truth and justice will more likely be achieved. In each trial that search begins with the selection of the jury.

Judge Maurice Braswell, a retired judge of the North Carolina Court of Appeals and a special emergency judge of the superior court, wrote a paper on jury selection in which he invited trial judges in their overseeing of jury voir dire to "rediscover and apply [sound] boilerplate principles of law as established by the North Carolina Supreme Court." I took that admonition very seriously. It is the duty of the judge to see that a competent, fair, and impartial jury is impaneled in each case he tries. I made a concerted effort to faithfully follow Judge Braswell's boilerplate principles.

Lawyers on both sides tend to resist the enforcement and application of these principles unreasonably and stubbornly, because they effectively place a bit and bridle on the trial lawyers. In one civil trial in Pitt County, an older and more experienced plaintiff's attorney seemed intent on ignoring principles firmly established in North Carolina law. The more I reminded him of the rules of *voir dire*, the harder it became for me to govern the proceedings. In frustration with the imposed restraint, the lawyer, at the bench, finally exclaimed, "Judge, all I want to do is try my case." To his protest I promptly replied, "You will be allowed to try your case within the boundaries set by the law, and no other way." My will prevailed, but only after threatening him that the twelve jurors then sitting in the box would be the jury and he would forfeit any further *voir dire*. As I had done on several occasions, I shared a copy of Judge Braswell's paper with the recalcitrant lawyer, even with the full realization that it has always been a difficult proposition to teach an old dog a new trick.

Whatcha Gonna Do?

The lawyers in a particular county are known as the county bar, and the lawyers who engage in trial practice are the most public representatives of the county bar. County bars, like individual judges, have their own personalities. And as with individuals, the personality can be considered more easily and assessed more clearly by the observer than by the possessor. While serving as a trial judge, it was my opportunity and honor to hold court in about forty-four of North Carolina's one hundred counties, even if my service in some of those counties was limited to one weekly term. Just like a one-time encounter with an individual person, it is difficult to make up one's mind about a county bar's personality during a one-week assignment. Of the counties in which I regularly held court, my favorite was Wayne County. The Wayne County bar was friendly, challenging, and courteous.

At the conclusion of an assigned six-month term in Wayne County, the presiding Superior Court Judge would be honored by the bar at a luncheon meal at a local restaurant. At this lunch I enjoyed a light roasting by the Wayne County bar, with the opportunity to respond in kind to the good-humored barbs. On one such occasion I was given a homemade greeting card signed by the various members of the Wayne County bar and the courthouse personnel. Inside the card the words, "Whatcha gonna do?" were printed.

They pointed out to me that I would say the words, "Whatcha gonna do?" several times during the court day. Anytime that there was a lull in the proceedings I would politely pierce the stillness with the question addressed to someone or another: "Whatcha gonna do?" The inquiry would quickly halt the hiatus and restore activity to the proceedings. The lawyers and the court personnel had noticed this habit of mine that I had failed to catch. I then commented upon some of the more frequent mannerisms and proclivities of the various trial lawyers who daily appeared in my court to bestow upon the bar its collective personality.

Part IV:
Tales from the Courtroom

A Judge

A judge should not fear making a mistake. He should not fear making an incorrect ruling or decision. He should not fear lawyers or be intimidated by bullies or blusterers. To use an analogy, a judge is much like a farmer who must go into his barn and care for his animals and manage their food and the implements used in his trade. A judge must go into his courthouse and care for those who are summoned to appear, to see that justice is offered and that cases are heard. Although there may be a skunk in the barn or in the courthouse, the farmer and the judge have no choice but to go inside and take care of business.

To fear making the required decision would be a dereliction of duty. A trial judge must decide and make the ruling or decision required based on the evidence before him and the law that he determines to apply. In most situations the trial judge does not have the comfort and convenience of taking his time or consulting others. A fear of failure or of reversal by an appellate court or a wish to avoid public controversy can paralyze the judge. In either case, the court fails to function with any fluidity and very little gets done.

During the mid-1990s, a murder trial was held in Pitt County. A very competent and experienced trial judge from a neighboring judicial district presided. The jury found the defendant guilty of first-degree murder. At the trial, the defendant was allowed, through competent counsel, to thoroughly examine the state's evidence and case. The trial judge allowed the defendant to cross examine the state's witnesses. The defendant presented his case without hindrance and within the bounds of the rules. The jury, chosen by the state and the defendant, unanimously found the defendant guilty of first-degree murder. The North Carolina Supreme Court, the state's highest judicial appellate tribunal, unanimously found that the trial was conducted without error.

Prior to the murder trial, one of the state's two female witnesses was severely assaulted by a gang of young girls who had been stirred to action by members of the defendant's family. Sometime after the defendant's conviction for murder, the young girls were convicted of the assault on the young witness. Considering the severity of the assault on the witness, the inherent integrity of the courts, and the faith that witnesses must have in the judicial process, an attack on this witness was a very serious matter. An attack on a witness called to testify in a court proceeding amounts to an attack upon the administration of justice in the community. Because this kind of assault and conduct must be deterred, I sentenced each of the girls to active prison sentences upon their convictions.

After the North Carolina Supreme Court reviewed the defendant's murder conviction and found no error, the defendant, through counsel, brought a motion for a new trial before the Pitt County Superior Court. The motion, which I heard, alleged that the young female witness, the one who had been assaulted (the motion made no mention of the assault), had now recanted her testimony given at the defendant's murder trial. The witness now gave testimony different from that which she had given under oath before the jury. At the hearing, I heard evidence about the assault that she had suffered and letters she had received from the defendant and his family. After hearing all of the evidence, I denied the defendant's motion to set aside his conviction of first-degree murder.

Before hearing the defendant's motion for a new trial, the defendant's lawyers moved that I recuse myself on the grounds that I had publicly offered my opinion on the subject of fatherlessness. It was and remains my opinion that the number-one underlying cause for escalating crime is fatherlessness. Somehow these very smart and sophisticated white lawyers linked fatherlessness with being black, and therefore concluded that the judge must admit that he was certainly a racist.

Often the occasion would arise when very smart and sophisticated lawyers would urge matters upon the court that were a stretch. And, upon very rare occasions, I would find myself regretting that I was a participant who had to listen to and consider their contentions. To hear them carry on and get past their self-righteousness sometimes seemed an impossible hurdle. It seems that it is an almost insurmountable task for such safe and secure people to own their biases and prejudices that they find so common in human beings of a more deplorable nature.

Parading Without a Permit

In my first spring as a trial judge, the district attorney for Pitt County called a case before me in which three codefendants were charged with parading without a permit. The defendants were accused of having organized a march without obtaining the necessary permit. This march was designed to call to the attention of the local authorities a grievance affecting the black community. The march and the subsequent trial had attracted much publicity, and the courtroom was crowded with onlookers interested in the trial.

Two of the defendants were local men, Bennie Boy Roundtree and King Gardner. Roundtree was a respected civil rights activist and the local leader of an affiliate of the Southern Christian Leadership Conference (SCLC). I knew both of these men fairly well. Both of them had waived their right to be represented by a lawyer and had chosen to represent themselves. The third defendant was Golden Frinks, a civil rights activist from Edenton and a

SCLC field secretary. I had first met Mr. Frinks almost twenty years earlier when I served as a law clerk for U.S. District Court Judge John D. Larkins, Jr. Robert White, a local, well-regarded attorney, represented Mr. Frinks.

The trial began with jury selection. Each of the defendants not represented by Mr. White was given a turn to question the jurors to determine their general fairness and competency to serve. Both of them asked suitable questions of the jurors and conducted themselves with appropriate dignity. Mr. White was one of the most highly respected members of our bar, and this case was one of the first of many that he tried before me over the ensuing years. He continues to practice law and is known to be a very good trial lawyer.

After the opening statements the state began to offer its evidence. The state's witnesses were individually called, sworn, and cross-examined by the defendants. Mr. Roundtree and Mr. Gardner conducted their cross examinations themselves since they each had waived their right to be represented by a lawyer. The two separately asked the state's witnesses very good questions and exhibited a fine attitude of respect for the adverse witnesses and the court process. Mr. White questioned the witnesses for his client, Mr. Frinks. Since each of the three defendants had the right to conduct his own cross-examination of the witnesses offered by the state, the state's evidence took more time than usual.

At the close of the state's evidence, the court informed the three defendants that each of them had the opportunity to offer their evidence. Neither of the defendants offered any evidence. The district attorney and the defendants were then given their turn to offer closing arguments. Since the defendants had offered no evidence, the district attorney argued first. He argued to the jury that they should easily find each of the defendants guilty of parading without a permit.

Each of the defendants then followed with their separate arguments, urging the jury to return a verdict of not guilty in their case. I gave the jury the standard jury charge for a criminal case and outlined the elements of the crime of parading without a permit. After the jury deliberations they returned the three verdicts. To my wonderment, the jury found Mr. Roundtree and Mr. Gardner not guilty of parading without a permit but returned a verdict of guilty in Mr. Frinks' case. The jury was formally discharged and I left them seated in the jury box.

The district attorney urged the court to give Mr. Frinks an active sentence of thirty days in the Pitt County jail, but Mr. White argued that an active sentence would be inappropriate. After the arguments of the lawyers about what sentence I should impose, I asked Mr. Frinks to stand. He stood and I asked him if he had anything that he would like to say to the court before I entered judgment.

He respectfully replied, "Judge, you just have to do what you have to do." I then said, "Madame Clerk, take this judgment. Upon the defendant having been found guilty by the jury of the misdemeanor of parading without a permit, it is ordered that the defendant pay the costs and a fine in the amount of fifty dollars." As the district attorney sat shaking his head silence came over the courtroom. After a few seconds Mr. Frinks looked up at me and asked, "Judge, did you just put me in jail?" "No, sir," I said. Then he replied, "Well, then I appeal." I then said, "Note the defendant's appeal, Madame Clerk," I then looked over at the district attorney and said, "Call your next case."

What's the Truth?

During the twenty-five years that I was a Superior Court Judge, I would estimate that I presided over more than 1,500 jury trials from call of the case to verdict and then judgment. I loved trying cases. It was always a pleasure to watch the jury work. On one particular Tuesday morning of a weekly term of criminal court in Pitt County, a case was called by the prosecutor. I cannot recall the charge against the defendant. A jury was selected, the evidence was presented by the state and the defendant offered no evidence. The lawyers argued the case before the jury.

After instructing the jury on the law that should be applied in the case, the jury was taken to the jury room to deliberate and instructed to knock on the jury room door when they reached a unanimous verdict. No more than five minutes passed and I heard a firm authoritative knock on the jury room door. I mentioned to Mr. Harvey that the jury must have a question. The bailiff returned and said, "No judge, the jury has a verdict."

I instructed Mr. Harvey to bring the jury into the courtroom and each of the twelve took their assigned seats. I asked if they had selected a foreman of the jury, and heads nodded. The chosen foreman was then asked to stand and identify himself for the record. The foreman stood. I then asked if the jury had reached a unanimous verdict and the foreman answered, "Yes, we have." He handed the verdict sheet to the bailiff and sat down in his assigned seat. The bailiff brought the verdict sheet to me and I examined the signed and dated verdict sheet and found it to be in order. The defendant was asked to stand.

The jury's verdict sheet indicated that the jury had found the defendant guilty. I read the verdict of guilty to the jury and asked, "Is this your verdict, so say you all?" All the jurors nodded affirmatively. I asked the lawyers if they had anything further with this jury and each responded that they did not. I then told the jury that they were released from their duties in the case and I asked them to remain seated so that they could observe the sentencing hearing portion of the trial. It was the shortest jury deliberation I ever experienced in my time as a judge.

As the jury sat in their seats watching and the defendant sat contentedly beside his lawyer at the defense table, I asked the defendant's lawyer if he had anything that he would like to say. He stood and respectfully pled for the defendant. He asked that his client be placed on probation and not be sent to the state's prison. After his remarks I looked over to the state prosecutor and asked if he had anything that he would like to say. He very eagerly responded, first, by reciting the defendant's lengthy criminal record. Next, he went on to tell me the various benefits to the citizens of Pitt County of having the defendant leave town for a year or two. He asked that I sentence the defendant to the state's prison.

When the state's lawyer had finished with his remarks, I asked the defendant to stand. The defendant stood behind the defense table. Allocution is the right of a defendant to make a statement before sentencing. The convicted defendant facing the judgment of the court is entitled to have an opportunity to address the court before the presiding judge pronounces judgment. As the defendant stood there behind the table, I asked him if he had anything that he would like to say. The man responded, "Yeah, I do, Judge. When I come in here yesterday morning, I knowed I was guilty. But, after what I heard my lawyer tell that jury, I ain't so sure." A middle-aged woman in the front row of the jury box folded her arms in disgust, in what seemed to me to be complete disbelief. It was interesting that, excepting the defendant, the defendant's lawyer had failed to convince anyone in the courtroom that the state may have failed to prove the defendant's guilt beyond a reasonable doubt. The jury was not amused. The defendant was sentenced to an active prison term.

Peeling Potatoes

The assistant district attorney called a case of an elderly woman charged with assault with a deadly weapon with intent to kill. He and the defense lawyer had entered into a plea bargain which provided for the woman to enter a plea of guilty to simple assault. As in each guilty plea offered to the court, the assistant district attorney was required to present to the court a factual basis to support the plea. The facts, as agreed to by the state's lawyer and the defense lawyer, were generally that the defendant was sitting on her own front porch in west Greenville with her daughter, peeling potatoes, when the alleged victim drove his Chevrolet Monte Carlo into the front yard.

After an initial heated conversation, the victim was told to leave the premises. He was a young man, apparently acquainted with the defendant's daughter. The conversation became increasingly heated and the victim was told by the defendant to leave her yard two or three more times. Finally, she told the young man that if he didn't leave that she was going inside her home and get her shotgun. He didn't leave and she left the porch and returned with a shotgun. As the woman walked onto her porch holding the shotgun, the driver of the Monte Carlo stepped back and stood behind the driver's door of his car. He was again told by the woman to leave her premises. He didn't. The woman fired the shotgun. The thick fresh mud from a large mud puddle just in front of his car covered the young man and his Monte Carlo. He left in a hurry.

The factual basis given to me by the district attorney was almost comical. I could see how that the defense lawyer might want to take the state's offer of the misdemeanor, simple assault, since his client was charged with a major felony. The woman was defending her property from an aggressive and persistent bully. The circumstances of the incident seemed to weigh in her favor. Accepting her plea of guilty to anything rankled my sense of what is right and just. It seemed to me that the young man received his due and the matter ought to stop there. I did not accept the tendered plea and, had I have had the authority to dismiss the case, I would have gladly and quickly done so.

Out With the Old and In with the New

Pamlico County gets its name from the Pamlico Indians, an Algonquian native people. The county borders on the Neuse River to the west and south and the broad Pamlico Sound to the east and northeast. It is a rural county with many people making their living on the water and others farming. Near the county seat of Bayboro are the headwaters of the beautiful Bay River. In the autumn of 1987 I sailed with my brother-in-law up the Bay River, enjoying the sight of its golden marsh grass on its banks, to the little town of Bayboro. We tied up our sailboat at a dock near the small bridge on the east side of the town.

Across the road on the other side of the bridge stands the Methodist Church. The sun was setting, and we could smell the appetizing aroma of frying fish coming from the fellowship hall of the church. Since Pamlico County was one of the four counties of Judicial District 3, this Friday evening was a great opportunity for me to hunt votes in my recently announced campaign for the office of District Court Judge.

While enjoying a delicious supper of fried trout there at the church fellowship hall, I learned that the Pamlico Hurricanes, the high school football team, had a local game up the street from the church. I had hit the politician's jackpot. After supper we walked the short distance to the football field. At the game the local judge cordially introduced me to several citizens. I met all the local "movers and shakers" and learned that the "Hurricanes" had been jokingly downgraded to the "Tropical Storms."

After I had won the election and was serving as a District Court Judge, I was assigned to hold court in Bayboro. The court was primarily a traffic and misdemeanor court, with civil and family court matters heard after the prosecutor had completed the criminal docket. At the morning recess a local lawyer approached the judge's bench and told me that he had a client who was seeking an uncontested divorce hearing and judgment. I reminded him that the custom was to hear the criminal docket first.

The lawyer pointed out his obviously very pregnant client who was standing in the crowded courtroom aisle. His client held her left hand underneath her belly and was looking down at what appeared to be a watch in her right hand. I asked what she was doing and he responded, "Judge, she's timing her contractions." He then explained that the baby was not her husband's and that she really wanted to obtain her divorce before the baby was born. Knowing that time seemed to be of the essence, I said, "Bring her up here and we'll get this matter heard and judgment entered." I examined the file and found everything to be in order and, after a short hearing, I entered a judgment granting her a divorce. She smiled with relief and thanked me for hearing her case.

Just before the lunch recess the same lawyer again approached the bench and asked, "Judge, do you do weddings?" There at the other side of the bar stood the very same very pregnant woman who had just been awarded a judgment of divorce. I reminded the lawyer that judges in North Carolina are not authorized to perform marriages. Sitting there on the bench, I said, "You know, a District Court Judge cannot perform marriages but magistrates can, and there's one sitting just here." The local magistrate was sitting in a chair to my left against the back wall of the courtroom.

I turned to the magistrate and asked him, "Jack, do you have time to perform a wedding now before we all go to lunch?" The magistrate smiled and answered, "Yes sir! It would be a pleasure, Judge!" We all adjourned to the magistrate's office on the hall behind the judge's bench. There in his office the very pregnant woman was lawfully (and just in time) married to the baby's father in a very delightful ceremony. With a broad smile she thanked the magistrate and happily announced that all was put right and that her child was to be born in wedlock to its true and *bona fide* father. The magistrate, the High Sheriff and I went off cheerfully and contentedly to a celebratory lunch and the newlyweds spent their honeymoon with a brand new little one.

The Orphanage Offense

In the election of 2000 two lawyers practicing in Pitt County and two incumbent judges, myself being one, each ran for one of the two contested Superior Court Judgeships in the county. I held one of those positions and was engaged in a campaign to be reelected. The two candidates who each received the two highest votes on November 7, 2000 would be the Superior Court Judges-elect to take office on January 1, 2001.

It happened that during the heat of the 2000 election campaign a young mother of two small children appeared before me, charged with the Class I felony of passing a forged check. At a sentencing hearing held on October 3, 2000, the young woman entered a plea of guilty pursuant to a plea bargain that provided that another Class I felony would be dismissed. As with all matters heard before the superior court, the proceedings were recorded by a court reporter.

At the sentencing hearing the young woman's lawyer presented her case very well and asked that I do something extraordinary and enter a prayer for judgment upon her plea of guilty. During the hearing it was determined that she had two small infants by two different males and lived with a new boyfriend who was not the father of either of the two children. With her two small children in the backseat of the car, a male "friend" had driven her to the bank to cash the check. Without her knowledge the friend had left the bank parking lot, taking her children while she was restrained in the bank after the bad check was discovered.

In a plain, straightforward manner her lawyer recounted the situation and also described her life and the circumstances in which she lived. It seemed that the young mother, who was addicted to cocaine, was having trouble taking care of her children and, at the same time, attempting to maintain a job at a local restaurant. Although her mother was present at the hearing and spoke, neither the lawyer nor his client offered to identify any relative or friend who could or would take this young woman in and help her care for her small children. She also expressed a yearning to do better and to improve her situation. I felt great pity for the young woman and her children.

I decided to follow the lawyer's recommendation and grant the prayer for judgment with supervision by a probation officer for one year. In my comments to the young woman,

I suggested that she might consider making different life choices as to her relationships and her attention to the Lord. She would not consider the possibility of temporarily placing her young children in an orphanage where the two children might have a more stable and nurturing environment. She did not express any great alarm or offense at the suggestion but indicated that she would not consider that option at the time. Having not imposed a judgment that would have given her a felony record and having wished her good luck, I watched the young woman exit the courtroom with her lawyer. I did not think any more about the case and heard the remaining cases before me on the criminal docket.

A few weeks later it came to my attention that *The Daily Reflector*, our local newspaper, would be publishing an article about the young woman's sentencing hearing and my audacious suggestion that she might consider placing her children in an orphanage until she could get her life together. Since I maintained a good relationship with the newspaper reporters assigned to our courthouse and I had not been asked about the hearing, it was my hunch this situation might involve politics. It occurred to me that someone supporting one or more of my opponents in the pending election, which was now less than a month away, could think that the voters of Pitt County might consider my counseling to the young woman ill-advised. It was my understanding that the newspaper had acquired a transcript of the hearing.

CALL YOUR NEXT CASE

Early on in my judicial career it had been recommended to me by an older and more experienced Superior Court Judge that I instruct my court reporters to inform me if an uninvolved party requested a transcript of a hearing in which I was the presiding judge. I always followed that good advice. So, straight away I went to the court reporter who transcribed the hearing. I could not imagine that my trust in her was misguided. When I had become the Senior Resident Superior Court Judge, this court reporter had been the first person I hired.

At our meeting in her office, she revealed to me that she had supplied the transcript to two lawyers. One of the lawyers, who had paid her $100 for the transcript, had assured her that her involvement would not be discovered. Upon my request she gave me a copy of the transcript of the hearing, a copy of the lawyer's letter to her, and his cancelled check. The lawyer's letter to her was dated October 17, less than three weeks before election day. The letter indicated that he expected an expedited delivery of the transcript. My court reporter was very sad and regretful. I knew the lawyer to be somewhat of a bully and expressed my understanding and my great disappointment in her.

After some thought about the situation, I visited my campaign manager Kenneth Dews, who was a good friend and a long-time trusted advisor. He agreed with my assessment that this was just part of the politics of the campaign. He also agreed that the overwhelming majority of Pitt County voters would find my advice to the young mother most appropriate. I then suggested to Mr. Dews that it would only be fair for the voters to be informed about the interest of the two lawyers and the political nature of their connivance. We determined to seek an audience with the senior editor of *The Daily Reflector*.

When Mr. Dews and I went to visit the editor, we sat down in his office and I asked him about the upcoming article. He seemed surprised, and not happily so, about our knowledge of the article and my awareness of his possession of the transcript of the sentencing hearing. I told him of my sincere appreciation for the paper's motto of "Truth in Preference to Fiction." I then asked if he intended to name the lawyers who, in the midst of a political campaign, brought to him their personal dissatisfaction with my remarks that had been graciously received without objection by the young woman and her lawyer.

The editor then protested that the confidential sources of the information would remain undisclosed. I then told the editor that I knew the two lawyers who were the "sources" and gave him my copy of the lawyer's letter to the court reporter and the lawyer's cancelled check. I suggested to him that the "truth" was that this was a political act in the midst of a campaign and that fairness dictated that the newspaper's readers get the whole truth. I suggested that if a "bunch of lawyers" who wanted to run the courthouse were attempting to somehow discredit the sitting judge, then the people might like to be informed of such a possibility and make up their own minds. The amicable meeting came to no resolution, and we bade the editor "good day."

Kenneth Dews, a survivor of the battle of Pearl Harbor, was a highly respected community leader. Having his quiet presence at the meeting with the editor assured the editor's reluctant yet honest consideration. A local newspaper, like most individuals, wants to appear to be fair in its dealings as it seeks to mask its bias and prejudice. The article was published, and the two lawyers were mentioned in the article.

Considering the many positive comments people made to my wife and to me about the article and the fact that on election day I received the most votes out of the four candidates, I feel very comfortable in claiming emphatically that the article helped me in the election. The common sense of the common man and the common woman, the informed voter, should not be misjudged or sold short.

It is in the people that I put my confidence to make the right decision. Whether sitting as a juror in a trial or going to the polls in an election, I trust the decision of the people when they are properly informed. It is with "the high and mighty" that I have misgivings and a sharp and decided lack of confidence. It is "the high and mighty" who sell short the capacity of the common man and woman to appreciate the truth. The truth is that the unmarried woman would have been better off to have temporarily placed her children in an orphanage until she was able to put her life back together. That's the truth.

Plead Guilty

It was Thursday afternoon of a scheduled week of criminal court in Wayne County, and the docket was complete. The assistant district attorney, the courtroom clerk, the court reporter, and the bailiffs were all present as we went over the week's calendar. Davis Harvell, a stern but gentle man, was a much loved and admired chief bailiff. He was always very aware of what was going on. While the assistant district attorney, the courtroom clerk and I were going over the calendar, Mr. Harvell left the courtroom and quickly returned with a young man following close behind. Mr. Harvell announced the man's name and explained that he had failed to appear at the calendar call on Monday.

I asked the young man his name and if he had a lawyer. He told me his name, looked me straight in the eye, and in a strong and assertive manner said to me, "Judge, all I want to do is plead guilty." I looked at the prosecutor who replied that, if the defendant would enter a plea of guilty, the state would not object to striking the order of arrest issued at his failure to appear on Monday. I then looked at the defendant and asked him if he had a lawyer, and he responded that he did not. Then he repeated, "All I want to do is plead guilty."

I then asked the defendant if he would like to have a lawyer to represent him in his case. His response was again, "All I want to do is plead guilty." I then informed him that I must go through the process of determining if he understood his right to be represented by a lawyer. He then replied, "Look Judge, all I want to do is plead guilty." I told him that I understood, but the law required that I go through the process of informing him of his rights. He looked anxious and very impatiently said, "Okay, but judge, you understand that all I want to do is plead guilty."

With his cooperation, I was able to get through the process of informing him of his right to an attorney, and he signed the required form. We then went through the plea transcript, during which he interrupted me anxiously to impatiently remind me that all that he wanted to do was plead guilty. The process was completed, the forms were signed, and his plea of guilty to the felony of possession of cocaine was accepted by the court and entered on the record. The defendant was then given a suspended sentence and placed on probation. He was very courteous and smiled as he thanked the prosecutor and me for accepting his plea. I then asked Mr. Harvell to escort him down to the probation intake office.

The young man had taken one or two steps, following closely behind Mr. Harvell towards the exit door of the courtroom. I called to him and said, "Hold up there just a minute." The defendant and Mr. Harvell turned to face me. I looked at the young man and said, "If you don't mind, would you please tell me why you were in such a hurry to plead guilty?" He looked me straight in the eye and replied, "I just didn't want to go before that Judge Duke!" The clerk, the court reporter, and the prosecutor all gasped in unison. I looked at the defendant and said to him, "I don't blame you, I wouldn't either!" When he had left the courtroom with the bailiff, he turned and peered through the small pane of glass in the middle of the door with his mouth wide open in astonishment. Mr. Harvell had told him that he had just been before Judge Duke.

Lawrence, The Jury Foreman

Lawrence, my oldest son, announced one day that he had received his summons to jury duty. It made me very happy that he would be able to observe his father at work and possibly play a direct role in my workplace. The day of his jury service arrived and, along with about fifty or sixty other Pitt County citizens, he took a seat in Superior Courtroom #1 with his fellow jurors and stood to take the juror's oath. Lawrence closely observed the proceedings. After having selected one or two juries for criminal cases on the docket, on Wednesday his name was finally called and he was chosen to serve on a jury. The defendant was charged with the misdemeanor of communicating threats.

The jury was introduced to the communicating threats case and it took us the rest of the day and into the next morning to hear the evidence. By early Thursday morning all the evidence had been presented to the jury. I could easily see that my son was paying close attention and was making a fine juror. I was very proud of him and grateful that the assistant district attorney and the defense lawyer had allowed him to sit on the jury. Around eleven o'clock the arguments of the lawyers had been given, I had instructed the jury on the law that they were to apply in the case, and the jury was sent to the jury room to begin their deliberations. Presently, there was the customary knock on the jury door indicating that the jury had reached a verdict.

Upon my request the bailiff retrieved the jury and escorted them to the courtroom to take their seats in the jury box. I looked at the jury and asked, "Ladies and Gentlemen, have you selected your foreman?" Each of them nodded affirmatively. My next question was, "Will the foreman please stand?" My son stood. I was mighty proud of him. I then asked him, the foreman, "Has the jury reached a unanimous verdict?" He responded, "Yes, sir." I asked, "Have you marked the verdict on the sheet and signed and dated the verdict sheet?" He responded, "Yes, sir." I then said, "Please hand the verdict sheet to the bailiff." After Lawrence handed the bailiff the verdict sheet I said to him, "You may be seated."

After I examined the verdict sheet and found it to be in order, I asked the defendant to stand. I then read the verdict sheet indicating that the jury found the defendant "Not Guilty." The jury was then discharged from their duties in the case, the defendant left the courtroom a free man, court was recessed for lunch, and Lawrence and I drove home to eat. On the way home I asked Lawrence about his experience. He said that when the jury was to select a foreman, they all looked at him and said that he must know something about all this and voted to elect him foreman. He then told me that the jury didn't find the defendant guilty because the state didn't prove that the victim, the defendant's next-door neighbor, believed that the defendant might carry out his threat. Wow! Was I proud of him!

Prayer Works

The Word of the Lord and His Presence ought not, indeed cannot, be excluded from the courtroom. In fact, the Word of the Lord is an everpresent power upon which oaths are administered and given with solemnity and purpose. The judge is at his best when in prayer, calling on the Lord for wisdom and order. The litigants are most at peace when calling on the Lord for fairness, mercy, and judgment. And there are thousands in our communities who pray daily for the courts and the judges and all that takes place in our many courtrooms.

For some reason I had the reputation of being a tough judge, and I was known to be particularly tough on defendants who were charged with driving while impaired by alcohol or other controlled substances. While holding court in Beaufort County Superior Court at the courthouse in Washington, the courtroom prosecutor called a driving while impaired case. It was on a Tuesday morning and the courtroom was filled with defendants, witnesses, and jurors. The defendant's lawyer was very well known in the county, a contemporary of mine and a lawyer who I considered a friend. For whatever reason the lawyer did not wish to try the case before me or in the presence of so many potential clients, and he made a motion to continue the matter. After excusing the jury and hearing the motion, which was opposed by the prosecutor, the motion was denied.

The trial proceeded. The defendant was a middle-aged man who seemed to be a typically law-abiding citizen. A jury was selected by the defense lawyer and the prosecutor and evidence was presented with no apparent or discernible defense. The trial lasted about three or four hours and ended that afternoon. The defendant was found guilty by the jury. At the sentencing hearing it was revealed to the court that the defendant, who had not testified, had a record with prior convictions for driving while impaired. I learned that the defendant was married and living in his home with his wife and his minor children.

I sentenced the defendant to two years and suspended the sentence with a condition that the defendant serve a ninety-day term of confinement in the Beaufort County Jail. The defendant left the courtroom in the custody of the bailiff to serve his sentence, and the defense lawyer immediately left the courtroom without comment. The next case was called by the prosecutor, and the week proceeded with trials and defendants entering pleas or otherwise disposing of matters on the calendar. I continued to think of the defendant who had been given an active sentence of ninety days.

Late Thursday afternoon the prosecutor announced that all the matters on the court's calendar had been addressed. While packing my computer and my trial notebook in preparation for my return to my home, I looked at the courtroom clerk and asked her if she remembered the driving while impaired case where I had sentenced the defendant to a ninety-day active sentence. She replied that she remembered the case and I then instructed her to change the judgment to a thirty-day active sentence. It was very unusual that I would remember or think about a case or an imposed sentence after the matter had been heard. Something told me that a thirty-day sentence was enough to punish the defendant, to help him pay much-needed attention to his life and young family. I went home.

A year or so later, while on my way to our home in Bath, I stopped to shop for groceries at the Food Lion in Washington. In one of the aisles a middle-aged woman very politely approached me and asked if I was Judge Duke. I smiled and responded that I was he. I thought that she must be one of the several jurors who would occasionally greet me and let me know how much they had enjoyed serving. In a very pleasant manner she surprised me by asking if, by chance, I might remember a driving while impaired case in

Beaufort County Court where I had sentence the defendant to ninety days and then changed the sentence to thirty days. I returned her pleasant smile and responded that I did remember the case. The nice woman there in the aisle at Food Lion then told me that she went to the same church as the defendant, and she told me his story.

She told me that the man I had sentenced had had previous driving while impaired convictions that he had never revealed to his wife or parents, who also went to the same church. She told me, that because he would not be returning home for a period of ninety days, he called his wife sobbing and told her of his prior convictions and the sentence that he would have to serve. She then told me, with praise to the Lord, that his wife had called their pastor and other friends in the church to pray for her husband and for their family. With a beaming smile, she told me that the pastor reported at church on the following Sunday that their prayers had been heard and the sentence had been reduced by the judge to a thirty-day active sentence. In a joyful spirit she reported that the man who I had sentenced had given up alcohol, had become a pillar in the church, and was teaching Sunday School. The Lord had had His way. I say, "Praise be unto You, Lord God, King of the Universe, who, in His own time, brings forth righteous judgment."

CALL YOUR NEXT CASE

The Criminal's Hard Work

Throughout history there has been a "criminal element" composed of those who choose to make their way through life stealing the property of others. This sort finds enjoyment in the taking of the prize. In many instances the wrongdoer is taught his delinquent trade by a family member or friend who also makes his or her way through life by seeking the easy dollar. This errant and unmanageable teacher introduces the recruit to the excitement of the chase and the sport of taking goods and merchandise belonging to others. Having never really experienced the satisfaction of obtaining something through an honest living, it is hard for such a malefactor to understand the insult endured by the rightful owner.

As a judge I had the opportunity to come into contact with many of these genuine thieves in the counties where I held court. I had a revealing dialogue with one of these fellows in Wayne County, when he stood before me charged with a string of felonious breaking and entering charges.

Each charge involved his participation with two or three codefendants in entering the homes of citizens of Wayne County and taking the things enjoyed by the homeowners. This young man was about twenty-five years old and had been convicted of like offenses in surrounding counties. Represented by a lawyer, he had decided to admit his guilt and to plead guilty to felonious breaking and entering pursuant to a plea bargain. The terms of the plea bargain provided that he would plead guilty to eight counts in exchange for the prosecutor's agreement to dismiss a number of other breaking and entering felonies.

As I listened carefully to the prosecutor's presentation of each of the charges to which the defendant pleaded guilty, I noticed that three of the counts involved residences with addresses in the same rural location. The defendant entered his plea of guilty to each of the eight counts. I then heard from the defendant's lawyer and the prosecutor, who laid out the defendant's lengthy criminal record. I asked the defendant if he had anything he'd like to say before I entered judgment and handed down his sentence. He expressed his exasperation for having been caught and then charged with so many felonies.

The defendant's open and matter-of-fact nature prompted me to ask him if he by chance remembered the three residences that I had noticed were located very near one another. He responded by asking if they were near a church, which he named. The jury pool was in the courtroom watching the proceedings and waiting to be called for the next trial. A number of people in the audience nodded their heads and, as I was facing them, I answered the defendant that I thought the houses were located near the church he had named. I then asked him if he would mind giving me a full description of how he broke into those residences, and he responded that he would be glad to.

The defendant then set about, in the full hearing of the entire room, to give me a detailed explanation of the breaking and entering of each of the three residences located on the rural road near the church. He told me how for two or three days before the break-ins he and his friends would ride up and down the rural road at different times of the day. They would observe the residences and the times of day that the people who lived in each house would come and go. They would note whether there were children who lived in the houses and when they would leave for school and return from school in the afternoon. By the end of the three days, they had determined when the husband and wife left to go to work and when they returned, explaining that it was very important that they not enter when the homes were occupied.

After the preliminary surveillance, the three figured that the best time for them to break into the homes was around nine o'clock in the morning. All three break-ins took place within fifteen to twenty minutes. They would back down the driveway in their white Ford Econoline panel truck, quickly exit the vehicle and dash onto the back porch, kick in the back door, and rush quickly to the master bedroom. One man would examine the top drawers of the chest of drawers in search of small firearms while the other would search shoeboxes on the closet floor for hidden pieces of jewelry. The room would be generally searched for firearms around the bed and between the mattress and springs. They would then quickly leave the home returning through the den, taking any electronics as they went.

As the defendant gave me the detailed narrative of how they committed the felonies, his lawyer stood beside him dumbfounded. To be certain that I understood him, the defendant then said, "And Judge, once you've got everything loaded on the van and you're on the road and out of there, you've got to find someone to buy the stuff. Judge, it's hard work!" At that the waiting jurors, and even some of the defendants waiting for their cases to be called, let out a collective gasp.

The Loyal Man

Progressivism and its standard bearer, Jim Crow, birthed a tidy and effective method, through burdensome regulation and licensing, to place the reins on the common citizen desiring to work. Before a regular person with a calling to be a hair braider or barber or plumber or electrician or doctor or lawyer could do their desired work, lo and behold, they must obtain a license from the state to do so. Almost every successful tradesman wants to limit competition. They welcome regulations that keep others out of their trade. "We must protect the public!" they cry. Before the world became so complicated, the common citizen was expected to protect himself, and if some con artist hoodwinked him then he could rely on the common law to provide a remedy. The community would soon know the tradesman's reputation and the unlearned, unscrupulous fellow would be run out of town.

On the Monday of a weekly term of criminal court in Lenoir County, the assistant district attorney prosecuting the docket called to the bar a middle-aged woman charged with selling spiritous liquors without a license. When the woman entered the bar I asked if she had a lawyer, and she replied that she did not. After informing her of her right to counsel and that the court would appoint her a lawyer to represent her if she could not afford to hire one, she declined and signed a waiver of her right to counsel.

The woman appeared to be very self-assured and wise to the ways of the world. After I had informed her of her rights, the prosecutor immediately asked her how she intended to plead and she indignantly replied, "I don't know how I plead, Judge. I ain't heard the evidence yet." The manner of her response revealed a bit of meaningful awareness of the courthouse. I directed the clerk to enter a plea of "not guilty," and she returned to the audience to await the calling of her case.

That afternoon, first thing after lunch, the prosecutor again called the lady's case before the court. Apparently having talked with the defendant during lunch recess, the prosecutor announced that she intended to enter a plea of guilty as charged to selling spiritous liquors without a license. I asked her again about her decision to plead guilty without the advice of counsel, and again she told me that she understood her right to counsel and to a jury trial but she had decided to plead guilty as charged. There were in the courtroom that day several fine attorneys, one of them a highly respected lawyer who knew the community of Kinston very well. I have always thought that he may have advised the lady defendant to enter her guilty plea to the misdemeanor.

As is required in all cases where the defendant enters a plea of guilty, it is the duty of the prosecutor to make a factual showing before the court. The prosecutor recites the evidence against the defendant and the defendant is given an opportunity to respond and give his or her side. The defendant then admits guilt. The tall, composed, and very serious woman before the court listened to the prosecutor and admitted to the facts as recited. The prosecutor described a house in a Kinston neighborhood that was known to be a place where local men and some women would gather. It was said that the men who frequented the house would play cards and checkers and also drink beer and spirituous liquors. It was apparent that the prosecutor was giving a description, well-known to most informed onlookers, of a "shot house."

Having grown up in the small town of Farmville, not far from Kinston, I was reminded as I listened to the prosecutor about the amusements and refreshments I had observed being offered and enjoyed at the local Farmville Country Club. My very own father had enjoyed playing gin with his friends there for many years. It was there at the country club that the men gathered to talk at their leisure of the affairs and business of their community and enjoy their games and refreshments. On the wall of the Farmville Country Club was prominently displayed a license to serve spiritous liquors. I was also reminded of my friend and mentor, James McKinney, who had a chicken restaurant, and who was known to serve alcoholic beverages without any license.

After the prosecutor had completed her recitation of the factual showing, I asked the defendant if she had anything to add or show to the court. She responded that she did not. I then stated that the court found a factual basis to support her plea of guilty to selling and serving spiritous liquors without a license and accepted the woman's plea of guilty. While listening to the factual showing I noted that the woman was married and that she and her husband owned or rented the house. Having found a factual basis, it was now a time for the prosecutor to assert or propose an appropriate judgment. The prosecutor maintained that such a place as described was a disreputable establishment that should be prohibited and that the court should enter a judgment expressing the community's disfavor by forcing the house to be closed. I then invited the defendant to tell me what she thought an appropriate judgment would look like. She indicated that she had nothing to say.

Having considered the facts before the court and the appearance of the measured and deliberate lady before me, I entered the judgment of the court. I ordered that the defendant's sentence was to be suspended on the condition that she pay the cost of court and a fine in the amount of $1,500. Upon my completion of the judgment the defendant politely and vigorously complained that she could not pay such a high fine. Knowing that none had been paid, I suggested to her that the fine was just an appropriate tax levy. Based on prior experience with such cases, I suspected that her loyal man would soon appear to pay the fine, and I told her so. She gave me a polite and knowing smile and took a seat on the side wall of the courtroom and soon left the courtroom with a wink. Her man had come to her rescue.

A Life Sentence for Driving While License Revoked

There are a few lawyers who will strategically bring a matter before a judge just before a scheduled recess. The all-important lunch hour is determined by custom and the presiding judge, and its time and longevity, usually an hour-and-a-half, should be predictable. The court staff, jurors, witnesses, lawyers, and bailiffs all rely on its scheduled time to make their plans. It is not sensitive or bright for a judge to abuse the scheduled time for lunch, so the judge should avoid being rushed to hear a matter right before lunch.

While holding a criminal term of court in Pitt County just before the 12:30 p.m. recess, an older lawyer, one judges tended to keep a close eye on, appeared in the back of the courtroom. The lawyer was moving quickly towards the bar with a middle-aged man and woman trailing in his wake. Into the bar he came and positioned himself behind the defense table with the man and woman at his side.

He began, "Judge, my client is charged with driving while his license is revoked. He's a working man. He needs to have his case heard so he can continue to go to work. He and his fiancé have three children." I interrupted, "His fiancé?" The lawyer responded, "Your Honor, may I appear before you after lunch and present this case in a light more favorable to the court?" I said, "Yes, you may." I then looked at the bailiff and said, "Mr. Sheriff, please recess court for lunch until two o'clock this afternoon," The bailiff sang out, "All rise." And in a moment or two we were off to lunch.

When court opened at two o'clock that afternoon the lawyer asked if he could come forward with his client. The district attorney nodded his head. The three of them again took their places behind the defense table. At that time the law in North Carolina was that if a person failed to appear on a traffic citation at the date assigned for the case to be heard in court, then after a number of days their driver's license would be revoked. For whatever reason the man standing beside the lawyer had missed his court date and now found himself in that position.

The lawyer explained all of this and was requesting a prayer for judgment disposition. The lawyer assured me that the original ticket had been paid off. The entry of a prayer for judgment by the court would basically forgive the defendant of the driving while license revoked violation upon payment of the costs of court. The lawyer then finished his remarks to the court with a request that he be allowed to present the defendant's exhibit number one, which he identified as the marriage certificate of the defendant and the woman standing beside him. She wore a broad, pleasant smile. The lawyer continued, "Judge, knowing your strongly held opinions about family and the man's obligation to be committed to his children, I advised my client and his now-wife to get married during lunch. And they did."

I then asked the happy husband and elated, almost giddy, wife a few questions about their children and their home and found that they had lived together for several years without being lawfully married and now had three sons. I congratulated them on their marriage. Upon the defendant's plea of guilty to driving while his license was revoked, I ordered that a prayer for judgment be entered upon payment of the costs, and I then remitted the costs as a wedding present from the state.

As I walked down the hallway of the courthouse to my office the next morning, I met another lawyer who was known to be somewhat grumpy. I greeted him, "Good morning, John. How are you doing this morning?" He replied, "I suppose that I'm doing okay Judge, but I just don't know what to think about you." In surprise, I replied, "John, what on earth do you mean?" He then said in a low hushed growl, "Judge, you're the only judge I know who'll give a man a life sentence for driving while his license is revoked."

Speeding to Court and "Fuzz Busters"

One week I was assigned to hold a criminal term in Carteret County, a beautiful coastal county. It was on the Tuesday of that week that I was driving to the town of Beaufort, the county seat of Carteret County. To get to Beaufort from Greenville it is necessary that you travel N.C. 43 South. N.C. 43 is a two-lane major road that has a lot of morning and evening traffic. Since N.C. 43 is a very busy road I was traveling about sixty miles per hour, sort of going with the traffic.

All of a sudden a Carolina blue Ford Mustang came up behind me at a fairly fast rate of speed. Because of oncoming traffic the driver could not pass me, and he consequently followed my car at a very close distance, close enough that I could easily see the two young blond-headed teens in animated conversation. Except for not being able to hear them, they could have been in my back seat. The driver continually edged out into the oncoming lane in several attempts to pass. Eventually he passed me and sped out of sight. The thought occurred to me that these boys were headed to court.

Upon opening the Carteret County Traffic District Court at 9:30 a.m., I was greeted by a packed courtroom with lawyers gathered around the assistant prosecutor's table negotiating their respective cases for their clients. I gazed around the courtroom to see if, by chance, I could spot the two young boys who had sped past me in the Mustang. Lo and behold there they sat, about midway to the left of the center aisle.

The morning progressed with various cases being called by the prosecutor. About 11 o'clock the prosecutor called a case, and the driver of the Mustang came forward and stood beside his lawyer. The young man stood there very confidently; he had been charged with speeding, and relying on the eloquent words of his lawyer, he entered a plea of guilty. His lawyer told me that his young client had graduated from high school that spring and was to enter college in the next few weeks. I listened intently as the lawyer told me that he had one previous speeding conviction and had learned his lesson and would not be driving in such a manner in the future. The lawyer asked that I enter a prayer for judgment continued upon payment of the costs. This was a disposition available to the court that would result in no conviction for the speeding violation.

After the defendant entered the plea of guilty and the lawyer had finished his remarks, I asked the prosecutor if he had anything to say or if the charging officer had any statement or any objection to my accepting the plea. There was no objection and nothing offered by the prosecutor or charging officer. I then turned my long gaze upon the young man and just looked at him for a few long seconds. I then asked the young speeder if he had driven a Carolina blue Mustang to court that morning. Startled, he looked at me and then at his surprised lawyer, who had turned to look at him. He replied that he had. I then asked him if he remembered coming up behind a gray Mercury Marquis traveling close to the speed limit. He sheepishly answered that he might remember. I then asked his friend to come up. I could easily see that these were the two young teens who had anxiously latched onto my bumper. I described his driving and his disappearance as he sped away down the road. His lawyer remained quiet.

"You know," I said to him, "your lawyer has asked the court to impose a prayer for judgment. Do you understand what that is?" He replied that he did and responded that it meant that he would pay the costs and have no record. I replied that he had it about right. "That's an extraordinary disposition and I hope that you understand that the court will have to think about that one for a while. So," I added, "I want you and your friend, if he likes, to go right over there (pointing to a bench inside the bar on the opposite side of the room) and sit while I think about this." The bench that I directed him to was full of people from the jail dressed in orange. When the hour for lunch arrived, I told his lawyer that his client could go to lunch and should be sitting on that bench when I returned for the afternoon session. At two o'clock the young speeder was seated there with his friend. At five o'clock I told his lawyer that the young man should be sitting in the same place when court opened the next day. I told him I was still thinking about the request for the prayer for judgment.

At the end of the next day, after all the cases on that day's calendar had been taken up, I called the lawyer and the young men up to the table and asked the driver if he had learned anything over the past two days. He very politely and respectfully answered that he had. I then asked him what he had learned and he replied that he was very sorry for his conduct and that he really did not want to ever come back to court. I granted his request for a prayer for judgment upon payment of the costs. He left the courtroom with relief.

At another traffic session of the Carteret County District Court, I was approached by a lawyer who told me that he had a young client charged with speeding. The lawyer told me that it was a high rate of speed, I think I recall eighty-plus miles per hour, and that his client was a young college graduate who worked for a local bank. He told me how this young man had grown up in a pretty poor neighborhood and had really done well for himself and was totally distraught about this serious speeding charge. He asked whether the court would consider entering a prayer for judgment upon the payment of the costs. I indicated to the lawyer that if the prosecutor was okay with this, and he assured me that he was, that I might give a prayer for judgment. He assured me that the officer was in agreement, and I was inclined to grant the requested prayer for judgment upon payment of the costs.

Presently the young banker's case was called before the court. The sharp-looking young man was dressed in a dark brown suit, and he entered a plea asking that the court grant his request for a prayer for judgment. After I heard from the defense lawyer and the prosecutor, I asked the officer if he had anything that he would like to say or add. The officer replied, "Judge, this is a fine young man and he's doing well at the bank. He was very polite to me when I stopped him. He has no prior record, and the only thing that bothers me is that he has a 'fuzz-buster' in his car." A "fuzz-buster" is a device placed in a vehicle to detect a radar operated by law enforcement.

I then looked at the young man and said, "That's not good. Is your car here at the courthouse?" He replied that it was out in the courthouse parking lot. I then told him, "I'm going to tell you what you must do in order to have the court enter a prayer for judgment. You must go out to your car in the parking lot and 'dance' on the 'fuzz-buster' in front of the officer. Do you understand me?" He replied, "Yes, Sir. I understand you and I'll do it now." I repeated, "You must destroy it." He smiled and said "Yes, Sir."

The officer and the young banker left the courtroom and, in a few minutes, returned. The officer reported that the 'fuzz-buster' had been destroyed and then said, "But Judge, that's not the worst thing. While he was smashing the 'fuzz-buster' one of his high school teachers came up and asked him what he was doing. Judge, he fully explained and was very embarrassed that she had seen him in that situation. He won't be up here anymore."

The Loosened Tie and the Revealing Dress

Calling him by his first name, I asked a lawyer, who had been called by me to the judges' bench, how he liked the tie that I was wearing that morning. A little surprised at my question, he responded "Judge, I think that you have on a very handsome tie." I then asked him if he liked the way I had it tied? Not recognizing where this conversation was headed, he replied, "I like your knot, Judge." I then asked my friend to try to make his tie look like mine. I told him that I wanted him to wear his tie tightly gripped around his neck while he was in the courtroom. I asked him if his opinion of me might change if I wore my tie loosely in the courtroom. He didn't answer that question, but he understood. The lawyer left the courtroom and shortly returned with his tie neatly in place around his neck.

On another occasion I found myself sitting on the elevated judges' bench pondering what I might gracefully do or say to encourage an attractive female lawyer to change her dress. That morning the court had convened and there she stood at the defense table wearing a very revealing dress. As the morning progressed, I began to notice the obvious attention that this woman drew. No one commented to me, yet I could see that the sight was appearing to divert attention away from the proceedings.

Finally, I thought of a way that I might solve this problem. I called my female bailiff to the bench. I said to my bailiff, "Have you noticed anything distracting this morning?" The bailiff gave me a knowing smile and answered that she had. I then asked her, "Do you think that right after we recess for lunch, you could speak to her alone and encourage her to wear a more modest dress to the afternoon session?" The very experienced bailiff responded, "Yes, Judge, I'll be happy to." That afternoon when we reconvened for the afternoon session, the female lawyer appeared in a dress that barely revealed her ears. The public gets its impression of the court system from the appearance of the way judges conduct themselves and enforce the rule of decorum for lawyers and other court personnel.

CALL YOUR NEXT CASE

A Pregnant Juror

It was a swelteringly humid August Monday, and we were holding a term of court in Pitt County superior court. It was now after lunch and the jury pool was in the courtroom ready for twelve of their number to be called to sit on the first criminal case of the week. After calling the case I asked, "Mr. District Attorney, do we need a jury?" He responded, "Yes Sir, Your Honor." I then turned to the courtroom clerk and said to her, "You may call twelve jurors into the jury box." The courtroom clerk proceeded to call the twelve prospective jurors, who came forth from the jury pool to take their assigned seats. I noticed that one of the jurors called was very obviously pregnant, and to me it appeared that the birth could happen shortly.

I introduced the defendant, the case, and the lawyers for the state and the defendant. I then instructed the prosecutor that he could examine the jury. While the jury selection proceeded he came to the pregnant juror but did not address her obvious condition, so I decided to ask her about her situation. I said, "Ma'am, it is obvious that you are pregnant." She very pleasantly responded that she was indeed. I then asked her, "When is your baby due?" The juror responded, "Judge, it could be any time now." I then said, "Well, I estimate that this case will take about two or three days. Do you think that I might ought to excuse you from jury duty?" She responded, "Oh no, Judge." Smiling, she said, "You see, I have three children at home who my mother is caring for, and it is so quiet in here and this courtroom is so cool and comfortable. I think I'm very capable of hearing this case." She stayed to serve and left, still pregnant, with the other jurors at the end of the week.

The Root Doctor

I was enjoying a short respite in my chambers before the afternoon session was to begin at two o'clock. I had taken great pleasure in a barbeque sandwich and Pepsi at the local barbeque restaurant down the street from the rural county courthouse. At the knock on the door of my chambers, I answered, "Come in." After respectfully peeking around the open door, my bailiff entered the room and in an open attitude of feigned disgust, said, "Judge, we've got a situation in the courtroom." After I asked him what was going on, he replied, "The family has done gone and hired a dadblamed root doctor, and she's in the courtroom sprinkling ashes all over the pews and chairs and stuff."

We were in the second day of a murder trial. Those jurors who were not outside the courthouse or still at lunch were in the jury room. We all were waiting for two o'clock, when we would be called back into the courtroom to continue hearing the evidence. I looked at the bailiff and asked incredulously, "A root doctor?" He replied, "Judge, the root doctor is a woman who lives right outside of town. She uses roots and bones and all sorts of stuff to call up spirits and do magic and whatnot." My bailiff did not reveal any incredulity. I asked the bailiff to tell me who was in the courtroom other that the root doctor. He told me that three or four jurors were in the jury room, the defendant was being brought up from the jail, and no one else was in the courtroom.

When I asked if the root doctor was making any mess in the courtroom, my bailiff replied with an air of assurance, "Judge, the other bailiff and I have everything under control. We're not going to let her make a mess in the courtroom. You can hardly tell that she's been in there." I determined that this occurrence was not all that strange and uncommon. I asked, "How many times has this happened here in the courthouse before?" "Oh, Judge, it doesn't happen all that often." He continued, "It's just important to some folks and, I reckon, it's best to let them sort of conjure up most any kind of help they feel like they can get."

I replied, "Well, tell her to be careful with the spirits she conjures up on the judge's bench. Tell her she's got to be through with her operations before folks start coming into the courtroom." Three days later the jury returned a verdict finding the defendant guilty of murder. I'm sure the root doctor did the very best that she knew how, but in spite of all of her noble efforts, the spirits that the root doctor called upon were unable to bring any benefit or consolation to the defendant. Reason and common sense prevailed.

PART V: LIFE WITHOUT FATHER

Their Names are Legion

I had not been a trial judge very long before I realized that a very significant percentage of the people who appeared in criminal court charged with a felony had one common characteristic. Most scholarly literature and my experience indicated that about eight out of every ten people charged with a felony, whether white or black, male or female, rich or poor, have had no significant relationship with their biological father.

I began to speak about what I observed in pulpits and at civic clubs, but found very little interest in the topic. In my talks about the subject of crime and its interconnection with fatherlessness, I made it very plain that I did not offer this information as an excuse for wrongdoing. It appeared to me that there were so many "fatherless" people appearing before me that it could be said that their name is Legion.

Not all people who have had no significant relationship with their biological father live dysfunctional lives. Amazing mothers, grandparents, uncles, aunts, coaches, pastors, teachers, and friends provide love and comfort to the fatherless, brightening their lives. Most fatherless people never see the inside of a courtroom, but the stories of the fatherless defendants who came into my courtroom were numerous and constant. I think often of this poem by Antwone Fisher:

> *Who will cry for the little boy?*
> *Lost and all alone.*
> *Who will cry for the little boy?*
> *Abandoned without his own?*
>
> *Who will cry for the little boy?*
> *He cried himself to sleep.*
> *Who will cry for the little boy?*
> *He never had for keeps.*
>
> *Who will cry for the little boy?*
> *He walked the burning sand*
> *Who will cry for the little boy?*
> *The boy inside the man.*
>
> *Who will cry for the little boy?*
> *Who knows well hurt and pain*
> *Who will cry for the little boy?*
> *He died again and again.*
>
> *Who will cry for the little boy?*
> *A good boy he tried to be*
> *Who will cry for the little boy?*
> *Who cries inside of me*

A Probationer's Friend in Lee County

I don't remember holding court in Lee County more than two times. One of those times I was assigned to a small courtroom to hear probation cases and take guilty pleas. During the week a young man charged with a probation violation appeared before me, having waived his right to counsel. The tall, slender man requested that his suspended sentence be revoked. He wanted to leave probation and serve his sentence in prison.

He said to me, "Judge, I did wrong. I did what I was accused of doing and I just want to serve my sentence. Waiting for this hearing, I had a few months to think about my situation. While I was in the jail a man from a local church came and visited me every day. Every day, Judge. This man introduced me to Jesus. I know you hear people tell you all the time that they have found Jesus in jail. I know, I hear it. But I did. I really did. I'm free, Judge. I'm free for the first time in my life. I want to go serve the rest of my sentence and get free of this place and live my life."

I looked at the man. I looked at his probation officer, who fully supported his request. I then told the man that I wanted to ask him some questions about where he grew up and who was in his family. He answered all my questions and then I asked him about his father. He responded, "Judge, I don't think I've ever seen him. I wouldn't know him if he came into this room. That's the problem. Every night before I fell asleep I'd think about him. And every morning when I woke up he'd be the first person I'd think about, and I didn't even know what he looked like. I wondered about him. A friend of mine and I would sit on a bench at Crabtree Mall and every time a man would come by, one of us would say, 'That one right there is my deddy.' It was a game."

Then he added, "You know, Judge, I think every man has a hole in his heart that must be filled by his dad. The man has a key to his heart that he ought to use to unlock his child's heart. And now, Judge, I found out that if the father doesn't use his key, then the good Lord has a duplicate he'll use if you ask Him." I listened to him, and then I activated his sentence. He left the courtroom to go to the North Carolina Department of Corrections to serve his time. He was a good man, a free man.

CALL YOUR NEXT CASE

The Father Who Showed Back Up

In one case, a man came forward when his case was called, stood there at the defense table to my left and entered his plea of guilty to the charge that the district attorney and his lawyer had worked out in the plea bargain. I went through the plea transcript with the defendant and determined that he was satisfied with his counsel, that he was in fact guilty to the charge to which he was pleading guilty, and that he understood and accepted the terms of his plea agreement. He was about twenty-four years old and stood about five-feet-ten inches or so. His lawyer was tall, over six-feet-five.

After the district attorney had given a factual basis for the plea, I turned to defense counsel and asked if the defendant had anything that he would like to offer. The defense lawyer then began to tell me about his client, the man standing beside him. The man remained silent as his lawyer grew bolder and more confident in his words. Earlier in the day and on many days before, the defense counsel had sat in my courtroom listening to one plea hearing after another as he waited his turn to stand by his clients. Over many days he had had the opportunity to hear the stories and hear my questions regarding the defendants' family situations and the revealed absence of fathers in their lives.

The defense counsel continued more forcefully as he proudly proclaimed, "And, Your Honor, this man standing by my side this afternoon has the most important man in his life here with him in this courtroom. This is a man who has stood beside my client and been his faithful guide. This man has been in the life of my client. Judge, my client has had the benefit of a father who has been there for him." The lawyer then requested that his client's father stand and a man seated on the third or fourth row of the audience stood and nodded. As the lawyer continued to focus on the father of his client, I began to realize that his apparent aim was to politely rebuke me in front of the crowded courtroom on my publicly stated opinions about the effect of the absence of fathers in these defendants' lives. While his lawyer continued to go on about the man's father, the defendant remained silent.

When the lawyer had finally finished his remarks, I looked down at the defendant's extensive criminal record. Before me was a defendant I could not recall having ever seen before. I had listened carefully to the strong words of his lawyer and had determined that he believed them to be true. As I looked up at the defendant and stared into his eyes, I decided to follow a hunch and to respectfully reveal to the lawyer and to those present the truth of the situation that in these few minutes had been revealed to me. After a few moments of complete silence, I asked the defendant, "Have you ever seen me before? Have you ever appeared before me?" The defendant responded, "No, your Honor, I have never seen you or appeared before you."

Continuing to gaze directly into the defendant's eyes and taking a real chance that I could be wrong, I then asked him, "This man who you say is your father, this man who stood in the audience a moment ago, when did he come back into your life?"

The defendant then looked down for a moment as the silence of the courtroom became more pronounced. He looked up at me with tears flowing from his eyes. As his lawyer looked down on him the defendant answered with a clear voice, "About six months ago." I then asked him, "How long had he been gone?" His lonely response was, "All of my life." Who would cry for him? He had been on a lonely, godforsaken journey, without a guide or constant companion, without protection, without provision. I entered judgment and sentenced him.

Two Marines

Around 2006 I was assigned to preside over a trial in Onslow County in which the defendant, who was a U.S. Marine, was charged with first-degree murder. The district attorney for Onslow County called as one of his witnesses the codefendant, a fellow Marine who was also charged with first-degree murder and had agreed to testify in exchange for a plea to a lesser charge and lighter sentence. The codefendant testified that he and the defendant went to a bar to have a few drinks with the general plan that they would take advantage of or rob someone, maybe a patron. At that same bar was an older man, maybe in his late sixties, who frequented the bar and was generally known as a harmless old drunk who wore a suit and came from an old Onslow County family.

While the evidence was being offered, the defendant sat in front of me to my right at the defense table between his two lawyers. When I looked at the defendant, in my line of sight I could see just over his head a middle-aged woman, the woman's husband and two teenage girls. These were the only people on the right-hand side of the courtroom. I presumed that these observers were his parents and his siblings.

The codefendant testified that on the night of the killing he and his friend befriended the victim at the bar and, with the promise of going to a party where there was plenty of free alcohol, enticed him to leave the bar and go with them in the defendant's pickup to the promised party. As the codefendant testified, I had in front of me his pre-sentence report. The report revealed that his parents had divorced when he was fourteen years old. The codefendant continued to testify that while seemingly heading to the party with the defendant driving, the defendant stopped the truck on the lonely dirt road and said that he thought he had a flat tire. The older man got out of the truck from his seat between the two Marines and stood behind the pickup with the codefendant.

The defendant got out of the truck on the driver's side, and while walking back to the rear of the truck picked up a baseball bat from the bed of his truck. The codefendant testified that the defendant, his friend, violently swung the baseball bat, hitting the older man in the head. He knocked the victim down and then continued to repeatedly strike his head. He testified that the man's blood splattered all over them. The two of them left the older man there in the road after taking his meager money and possessions.

During the codefendant's testimony and the testimony of other state's witnesses that included the display of a group of horrific photographs, the defendant exhibited no emotion of any kind that I was able to observe. The defendant was found guilty of first-degree murder. Before entering judgment and sentencing the defendant to the mandatory life sentence, I addressed him and gave him an opportunity to speak. He declined to speak, and then I asked him if the man and woman and two teenagers in the audience were there for him.

Although I had never seen him have any communication with them during the trial, I asked him if the woman was his mother. He responded that she was. I then asked him if the man was his father. Until this question the defendant who had shown absolutely no emotion looked me straight in the eye. With that question his eyes glazed over, and visibly shaken, he responded that the man in the courtroom was not his father. His mother held her head bowed in her hands and she wept silently. The defendant then said, "My father left me when I was fourteen."

The Boy and the Dollar

On one Thursday the Pitt County district attorney called a case for a jury trial. It was apparent that the young defendant did not have a lawyer. He was charged with felony simple possession of heroin. I sent the jury pool out of the courtroom so that I could determine the status of the defendant's case and offer him another chance to have the court appoint a lawyer to assist him with his case. After reading the defendant his rights and reminding him of his right to counsel, he declined counsel and told me that he wanted a trial by jury. He planned to represent himself.

I had the bailiff bring the jury pool back into the courtroom, and the state's attorney and the defendant selected a jury to hear the case. The defendant was convicted of one count of simple possession of heroin. Before judgment and sentencing, the district attorney informed me that the defendant would enter a plea of guilty to an unrelated felony possession of heroin. I left the jury in the box to observe the judgment and sentencing procedures of the court. The state presented a factual showing for the additional case to which the defendant was pleading guilty.

The defendant, the state's attorney, the court reporter, the courtroom clerk, the two bailiffs and I were the only people, other than the jury, in the courtroom. The defendant was asked to stand and he politely stood. I asked him if he had anything that he would like to say, and he said he did not. The following exchange then took place:

Court: "Please tell me about yourself."

Defendant: "What do you want to know, Judge?"

Court: "Where did you grow up?"

Defendant: "I was born in Kinston and then went to Baltimore with my mother."

Court: "Do you have any brothers or sisters?"

Defendant: "I have one brother and one sister. My sister lives in Baltimore and my brother is in jail in Washington, D.C."

While the defendant and I were talking, the twelve jurors were all turned to their left listening intently and observing the defendant. In the middle of the back row of jurors sat Juror Number 10, a middle-aged man who had worn a cowboy hat to court and seemed to "mean business." What came next took everyone by surprise.

Court: "Tell me about your father."

The defendant had looked me straight in the eye as he answered my previous questions, but when I asked about his father his head dropped. He looked up at me, paused, and stood there quietly for a second. One shiny bright tear floated slowly down his right cheek. The jurors were in stunned silence and the courtroom was so still and quiet you could hear a pin drop. Quietly he said, "He gave me a dollar when I was four." Everyone in the courtroom was moved, especially Juror Number 10, who put his hands on his forehead and covered his eyes.

PART VI:
A Judge on the Road

A Judge's Southern Dinner

Northampton County is a beautiful rural county situated about seventy miles due north of Pitt County which shares a portion of the southern border with the Commonwealth of Virginia. The county seat, Jackson, is a small town of less than five hundred people. The county courthouse is a beautiful Greek Revival building situated very near N.C. 158, which is the "main street" of Jackson. Because of the need to cool the courtroom we would open the broad front door, and we could hear eighteen-wheeler log trucks roaring by.

In the little community of Jackson, one can find very few places to eat lunch. Many days we would join the sheriff in his office across the road from the courthouse. It could be most anything, and I really did not know where the food was coming from. Some days I would join the lawyers and we would walk down the street from the courthouse to a little sandwich place.

One day the sheriff asked me if I would like to ride over

to a place near the town of Seaboard with him to have lunch. We drove north out of Jackson through the countryside. This is a beautiful part of eastern North Carolina. The deputy slowed and turned into the yard of an old white clapboard building in need of painting. There was no sign of any kind on the outside of the building. We parked in the thick summer grass beside an old car near the structure, and I followed the sheriff and his deputy into a door on the right side. It was sort of dark when we entered the building, but as my eyes adjusted I saw a woman tending a stove behind a counter that was filled with every "southern" soul food that I loved.

My mother grew up in Centerville, North Carolina, and no one's cooking could match that of her or her mother. Except here, in this little building north of Jackson near Seaboard, I had found a wonderful fountain of just plain good food that tasted just like the dishes prepared by my mother. The three of us sat at a table in a small, fairly dark room, and the woman doing all the cooking also did all the serving. The sheriff seemed to know her well, and we enjoyed a very memorable meal.

We returned to the courthouse and finished the court on Friday, and two summers passed. I returned to Jackson to hold court, and again the sheriff asked me one morning if I would like to go back over to Seaboard and have lunch with the lady in the little white building. Of course, I enthusiastically replied that I was very interested to go back.

We drove through the countryside on a hot summer's day, and the green fields of corn and soybeans looked the same as they had looked two summers before. As we slowed to turn into the yard of the building I immediately noticed that the small little building was brightly painted white.

Outside, to the right of the building, were two F-150 Ford pickups, one red, the other blue, and a white Cadillac Escalade. The inside of the building did not seem to have changed very much. The food was still very delicious. What had changed was that the woman who still did the cooking and serving had won the lottery and now had a lot of money. The sheriff told us how she had bought each of her children a Ford F-150 pickup and she had bought a Cadillac Escalade for herself. The woman had kept her desire to serve others and to give out of her abundance.

Barbecue

About three o'clock in the afternoon sometime in the summer of 2000, Martha Roberson, my judicial assistant, peeked her head in the door of my chambers and said, "Judge, there's a man from *The Washington Post* on the phone." I said, "Really? What on earth do you suppose he wants to talk about? Patch him through!" The fellow on the other end of the line began the conversation by saying, "Judge, I hear you like barbeque." He identified himself as Adam Platt with *The Washington Post Magazine*. I said, "Yep, I really like barbeque. I eat barbeque for lunch at least twice a week." Mr. Platt was a very friendly fellow. "Where'd you hear that I like barbeque?" I asked.

Mr. Platt then told me that he had travelled across North Carolina from east to west sampling barbeque at the most renowned barbeque restaurants and he was writing an article on North Carolina barbeque for *The Washington Post Magazine*. He told me that my name had been mentioned at barbeque restaurants in Greenville, Goldsboro, and two or three other towns. We began a delightful conversation about one of the most favorable delicacies in all this world: eastern North Carolina barbeque. We laughed about how most northerners think of a gathering of neighbors where meat is cooked as a barbeque. Southerners, on the other hand, call that a cookout.

Then Mr. Platt asked me which barbeque I liked the best. I became quiet and hesitantly replied, "Now, we're getting into a really personal matter. When you're talking about barbeque it becomes very personal. And political." I told him that I could not answer that question. I explained, "When you have to run for office down here in North Carolina, you don't give your opinion as to your favorite barbeque. You can lose votes taking the wrong turn on that question. So we politicians tend to keep quiet and eat our food." We laughed and talked a few minutes more. In September I received two copies of the latest issue of *The Washington Post Magazine* featuring Platt's article entitled, "High on the Hog." There are some really great barbeque places in Greenville, and I personally enjoy being served barbeque at each of those fine establishments. And that is all I have to say about that.

A Leg Pulled in Warrenton

On the Duke side of my family all my people are from Warren County, so being assigned to hold court in Warrenton, the county seat of Warren County, was a special event for me. The Clerk of Superior Court was a special friend who was married to a girl from my hometown, Farmville. Growing up I would spend several weeks each summer with my maternal grandparents in Centerville, a crossroads eighteen miles south of Warrenton. A trip to Warrenton with my grandmother was a very special treat.

Having spent the Sunday night before the Warren County superior court term with a cousin in Centerville, I arrived in Warrenton a little over an hour before court was scheduled to convene. It was a beautiful warm early summer morning in an idyllic North Carolina small town. I walked from my parking place across the courthouse grounds towards the bustling downtown. Although it was not as busy as I remembered when I was a child, there were still a lot of cars on the street and people going to and fro. I joined the people walking down the brick sidewalk.

There, on Main Street, stood W.A. Miles Hardware. It seemed to me that I had been here at another place in time. As I walked nearer to the old store a tall lanky man came out of the prominent storefront rolling a bicycle, which he placed near the entrance on the sidewalk. He reentered the store only to emerge pushing a wheelbarrow, which he rested on the brick sidewalk near Miles Hardware's tall front door. The friendly old man and I entered the old store laughing and talking together. The store was, in my mind, a classic hardware store. It had a tall ceiling with old globe light fixtures hanging by long chains which dimly lit the various items and implements for sale.

From the store's entrance the aisle curved to the right and to the left. My natural inclination was to follow the right. The aisle led me from the entrance to the rear of the store, revealing to me the sights and sounds of an old hardware store. It was full of shovels, rakes, pocketknives, plumbing pipes, electrical wires, and everything else one could imagine a modern person could need. The store had tin doll houses and model service stations with cars up on high shelves. It was a fully operational American museum of life, but it sadly recalled a dying era. It was a very special place, and I knew that I had visited there with my grandmother a half-century earlier.

It became apparent that the aisle was in the shape of a horseshoe. Following the aisle, one would travel around the back portion of the store and eventually return to the front door, which was now wide open. About halfway down the left side of the store I was joined by Mr. A.D. Johnson, the proprietor. Mr. Johnson was a fairly tall affable man, slender in stature, probably around sixty to sixty-five years old. He greeted me in a very friendly manner common in North Carolina. We began to visit as we walked down the aisle towards the front door. As the aisle curved to the left to go out we came upon an old worn-out baseball mounted with a screw through a two-inch wooden block. The baseball sat there on the crowded counter, its leather cover now partially black and its stitching worn off in places. It looked like every person in Warren County had touched that baseball.

"What's the significance of this baseball?" I asked as Mr. Johnson walked down the aisle next to me. "It looks like every finger in the county has rubbed this baseball. How old is it?" Mr. Johnson looked at me with the reverence of a Baptist preacher on an afternoon walk through the church graveyard. "That's the last baseball Babe Ruth hit over the left field fence in Yankee Stadium," he answered. We just stood there in silence.

I was dressed in a dark blue suit and wingtips. Having never seen me before in those parts, Mr. Johnson had determined that I was in Warrenton for court that morning and guessed that I was the judge. When he told me that the baseball was Babe Ruth's last baseball hit over the left field fence in Yankee Stadium, I asked in astonishment, "Does the Yankee organization know you have it? Why don't you keep better care of it?" As I continued my examination of Mr. Johnson, the tall lanky old man came in the front door from the sidewalk and asked me, "Is Mr. Johnson lying to you about that old baseball?" As I turned to Mr. Johnson he gleefully said with a great big smile, "You know, for a judge, your leg is mighty easy to pull!" I looked at him with a smile and said, "Yep, that's why we have juries, because it is mighty hard to pull twelve legs at a time."

Not long after my term in Warren County Mr. Johnson sent me a new baseball signed by him with a note, "Judge Duke, don't forget Babe Ruth's last home run ball." For several years thereafter, Mr. Johnson would send me delicious Ridgeway cantaloupes grown in Warren County.

Driving to the Courthouses

Being a circuit judge meant driving to courthouses that are an hour or two from my home. Eastern North Carolina is quite rural and there are not many places to spend the night. Pitt County was one of twenty-two counties in the First Division. Currituck County and Dare County were the only counties where I almost always spent the night, and occasionally I would also stay over in Pasquotank County.

The drives to and from the various courthouses were very enjoyable. Each morning and evening I would take pleasure in the sights of the countryside. People were going to work or farmers were in their fields, or some folks were just sitting on the front porches of modest houses near the rural roads. Each morning and evening would bring new bucolic glimpses of rural life. During the early morning trips the world would be awakening to a new day, and in the evening returning to rest. Before leaving home I would set my Garmin GPS to determine my arrival time to court.

I determined early on in my tenure as a trial judge to give myself ten minutes or so at the courthouse before court was scheduled to open to visit with bailiffs, lawyers, or clerks and to begin court on time.

On one of my morning drives to Halifax County to hold court, while driving just south of Scotland Neck and listening to David Jeremiah on the radio, I witnessed an astonishing sight. Along both sides of the road approaching the small town of Scotland Neck from the south are large fields. As I was driving down the pleasant road, I could not believe my eyes as an ostrich ran along side of me about fifty feet from the road. He seemed determined to keep up with me, so I slowed my car and for about a mile the ostrich and I enjoyed the sport of "racing." It was an unforgettable sight and experience. He seemed to appreciate my slowing my car down and giving him leave to keep pace with me and entertain himself with the competition. He must have realized that I enjoyed the chance engagement as much as he seemed to.

One morning I was traveling north on N.C. 11 to Winton, the county seat of Hertford County. It was a clear day and the sun shined brightly in the cool early hours of the day. The court session had gone well and I was returning for the week's last day of court. The fall air was so comfortable that my driver's side window was open and, except for my car and the occasional fellow driver, the world stood in quiet stillness. Tall stately green pine tree forests stood on each side of the highway.

All of a sudden, out of nowhere, a jet, flying just barely over the tall pine trees, crossed the road immediately in front of my car. The sound of the low-flying jet was so fierce and the crossing so immediate and unexpected that I almost lost control of my Mercury Marquis. After driving a mile or two down the road and totally shaken to the core, but recovering, the first pilot's wingman performed the very same maneuver. Again, I was shaken to the core. I imagined the pilots talking to one another over their mics. They both had to have had a hardy laugh. It was the sound of freedom, up close and personal.

One evening while returning from court in Northampton County, I came upon a car and an eighteen-wheeler truck sitting stationary in a curve. In the twilight I could see that there had been an accident. The truck was on the inside of the curve about halfway off the road, and the front of the car was resting against the left front wheel of the truck. There were one or two other cars that had stopped to lend assistance, and I stopped and got out of my car and walked to the scene. No ambulance or highway patrolman had arrived. I was greeted both by a woman who had stopped and the distressed truck driver.

The truck driver sorrowfully shared with us that the driver of the car had apparently fallen asleep, that he could see from his moving cab that she was asleep when she crossed the centerline. The driver of the car was sitting erect in her driver's seat with no visible sign of injury. She seemed to be just sitting there waiting. The woman who had stopped told me that she was a nurse. The truck driver was heartsick as he quietly told me that the driver of the car was dead. The nurse looked at me and nodded. We all knew that somewhere along this road there were loved ones who would be heartbroken.

The morning and afternoon drives to the courthouses were a great gift to me. The morning trip gave me a chance to think about the approaching day to be spent in court and to contemplate my role as the judge. The afternoon return home gave me a chance to reflect on the day's work and the case or cases awaiting my return to court the next day.

Mattamuskeet School and the Second Grader

Hyde is a wild, isolated and sparsely populated county on the north shore of the large Pamlico Sound in eastern North Carolina. Hyde County includes Ocracoke Island, the most isolated place in North Carolina and one of the barrier islands between the sound and the Atlantic Ocean. Including Ocracoke Village and three mainland villages—Englehard, Fairfield and Swan Quarter—Hyde County has two, maybe three, caution lights in the entire county. Fairfield is a small village on the north side of Lake Mattamuskeet and at the top of the causeway that transverses the large shallow lake. At the south shore of the lake is Mattamuskeet School. Engelhard and Swan Quarter are two small fishing villages along Highway 264 about fifteen to twenty miles apart. Swan Quarter is the county seat, where a small courthouse housed the upstairs courtroom.

Hyde County would have two or three sessions of criminal superior court in a year. It was always a busy full-term court for me. Citizens from all over the large county and the island of Ocracoke would gather there as jurors and defendants, and we would try several cases during the week. One week the sheriff told me that the folks out at the school wanted to fix me a fried seafood lunch, and asked me if Wednesday of that week would be okay. Being eager to taste some great seafood and meet the people at the school, I readily accepted their kind invitation.

On the appointed day the Sheriff, the Clerk of the Superior Court, the Register of Deeds, my bailiff, and I drove the short distance from Swan Quarter to the school for lunch. We were greeted at the schoolhouse front door by the principal, two or three grammar schoolteachers and a reporter from the *Washington Daily News*. Washington is the small town located up the road in neighboring Beaufort County. We all went straight to the lunchroom where we enjoyed a delicious platter of some of the freshest and tastiest seafood in all the world, served with slaw and stewed potatoes. While we were having lunch and enjoying the conversation, I learned that the plan was for me to meet some young elementary students in the school gymnasium.

After we all had finished our lunch, we walked a short distance down a hallway and into the gymnasium. On the gym floor were small children going through their calisthenics. I was encouraged to join in with the children, and I gladly did so. I performed the exercises they were doing, and I was really having a good time. The principal and teachers and all the courthouse officials seemed to be more reserved than I was, and they happily watched as I did the calisthenics that the children did.

Some more children entered the gymnasium, and the principal interrupted the activities and told me that each of the children would like to shake my hand. I readily agreed and the schoolchildren lined up to shake the judge's hand. As I greeted the children on bended knee, each child filed by me. I could look each child in the eye as I greeted them. Most did not have anything to say. Standing immediately behind me were the principal, three or four teachers and the newspaper reporter, who was listening carefully and taking pictures. A small boy stopped in front of me. When I shook the young lad's hand, he looked at me in sort of a way that seemed sad and said, "I had to repeat the second grade." I thought, "Why are you doing this, Lord? How do you want me to respond?" In a flash I looked the boy straight in the eyes and said, "That's okay, it's alright, that's nothing. I repeated the second grade too! I'm now a judge. You can do anything you want to do if you work hard."

At that, one of the teachers behind me exclaimed, "Judge, you flunked the second grade?" I turned to look up to the principal, the teachers, and of course, the newspaper reporter, and said, "Yes, I did. It's one of the best things to ever happen to me." For many years I had been secretly ashamed of my failure. When friends or others would judge or write off their fellow man because of something that person did or didn't do, because of their failure, I used to stay quiet. That little boy set me free of my shame.

JUDGE RUSTY DUKE

THE TOP OF THE COURTHOUSE

As a circuit judge it was my privilege and pleasure to meet and get to know some very interesting and well-liked people in many different counties. The elected clerks of court all stood out as dedicated public servants who aimed to please the public, the lawyers, and the visiting judges. Depending upon the population of the county, the clerk's offices had as few as three or four deputies and assistants to as many as fifty or more. The county clerk of superior court is an *ex officio* judge responsible for the filing and safekeeping of public records and papers regarding almost every aspect of human living.

Tyrrell County is a rural county situated between Washington County and Dare County in one of the most sparsely populated areas of North Carolina. Tyrrell County is reputed to have a greater bear population than human population. It is a very pleasant place, and at that time only one lawyer lived and worked in the small town of Columbia, its county seat. Lawyers from the adjoining counties would come over to Columbia to ply their trade and lend an opposing side to its sole hometown lawyer. The old courtroom was on the second floor. A narrow unimposing stairway led to the small yellow painted room with portraits of old lawyers hanging on its walls. A small judge's bench faced the entrance to the room with two small tables for counsel facing the bench. A picket railing separated the public from the working area within the bar. The door to the small jury room opened from the courtroom, and if deliberations became heated they could be easily heard in the courtroom.

While presiding during one of Tyrrell County's four annual criminal terms, the prosecutor called a "bear case" in front of me. Two defendants were being tried for taking a bear by illegal baiting. The case happened to be well-known throughout the county. After hearing all of the evidence and the lawyers' arguments in the case, the jury was sent to the jury room to deliberate. After a few minutes, it became apparent that the sounds of the deliberations reverberating through the courtroom would prevent any further court business that afternoon.

I postponed all other matters on the docket until the following morning, and the clerk of the court and I grabbed two chairs and went out through a second-floor door to the top of the front porch of the courthouse. From our perch on the roof of the porch, we could observe all of the "goings-on" up and down Main Street. The clerk and I enjoyed the beautiful day seated beneath a large sign that read: "Tyrrell County." The conversation centered around Tyrrell County and its rich history in colonial North Carolina. As we talked we had occasion to visit with various residents who knew the clerk very well and stopped to holler up to us about how they had never seen anyone sitting on the roof of the courthouse porch. The clerk would explain that the jury was deliberating on the case at hand, that the judge needed to be nearby to answer any potential questions, and that this was a good place for the judge to smoke his cigar. In an hour or so the bailiff poked his head out of the door to the porch and said, "The jury has a verdict." We returned to the courtroom and justice was done. All in all, it was a good day.

A Good Man and the Farmville Christmas Parade

There was a man who lived in my hometown of Farmville who was known and liked by many of its citizens. I liked him and he, I think, liked me. Every year, around the first or second week of December, the Farmville Christmas parade would take place. As one of the elected officials of the county, I would be invited to ride in the parade. My wife and I owned a 1975 Carolina blue Buick convertible, and each year we would dress it up with two magnetic signs displaying my name and office and a big red velvet bow for the hood ornament.

One year, in the early 2000s, I took my assigned place in the parade behind an esteemed local member of our state legislature. I was riding in the back seat of my shiny Buick convertible. I loved the Farmville Christmas parade, and on several occasions I would invite a young nephew or niece to accompany me. As I slowly passed the First Christian Church down a very crowded Main Street, I heard a familiar voice shout, "What d'ya say, Judge?" My head turned and I saw my friend Bobby standing in the crowd in front of the church. He wore his familiar grin and I could see his prominent gold front tooth. I smiled and blurted out, "What are you doing out, Bobby?" And the parade onlookers all laughed and howled. It had not been long that I had had the unpleasant task of activating Bobby's six-to-eight-month suspended sentence because he had committed a probation violation.

When my segment of the parade had completed the parade route, I walked among the crowd hoping that I would run into Bobby. I felt very bad that I had responded to Bobby's happy greeting in the manner that I had. So, while the remainder of the parade proceeded and Santa Claus rode atop the fire engine down Main Street, I saw Bobby and crossed the street to talk with him. I wanted to know how he was doing; I told him that I should not have said what I said in front of so many of his friends, and I told him I was sorry. He responded, "Hey, Judge, that won't nothing." We both laughed and went our separate ways.

The next year I returned to Farmville to again take a place in the annual Christmas parade. I had not found a driver for my car and when I was about to get into the car and drive it myself, it seemed that out of nowhere Bobby appeared. I caught his attention and asked him if he would drive me in the Christmas parade. He grinned and very happily agreed. I did not ask him if he had a driver's license.

My allotted slot in the parade approached, not too very far from the front of the parade. Bobby and I joined the parade behind the elected Pitt County Register of Deeds, and we proceeded very slowly down Main Street. As Bobby drove at the slow pace of the parade, we were both greeted with Christmas cheer from the many great citizens of Farmville. He would turn around and talk with me as he drove. As the Buick convertible approached the intersection of Main and Wilson Streets, the parade announcer introduced me and then recognized Bobby as my driver. Other than the time I rode with two of my very young children in the 1981 Christmas parade as mayor of the town of Farmville, I do not think I had had a better time in the Christmas parade.

As we slowly proceeded down South Main Street, I noticed that almost everyone seemed to know Bobby. He was smiling and keeping just the right distance from the car in front of us. We were having a great time. As we turned right onto Cotton Street, we both realized that the parade was about over for us. As we approached my parking spot at the town administrative building, I said, "Bobby, that was so much fun, why don't we get back into the parade and do it again?" Bobby hesitantly agreed, and we drove a few feet up to Main Street.

The parade was about at its midpoint. After we explained to the parade assistant that we would like to get back into the parade, he smiled and let us in. And off we went for a second time down the parade route. Once again we had a delightful time as we passed the astonished celebrants and enjoyed lots of laughs. Everyone seemed to delight in seeing us again. I enjoyed many a laugh with friends and family about that Christmas parade.

CALL YOUR NEXT CASE

PART VII: FINAL THOUGHTS

An Oath for the Lawyers

When I became the senior resident judge for Pitt County in 1993, the first full year that I served in that position, I decided that recently qualified lawyers, upon their admission to the bar, ought to be offered a comparably dignified swearing-in ceremony as judges are offered when they take their oath of office. An appropriate ceremony was scheduled and invitations were extended to all new lawyers and their families to attend the special swearing-in and admission to the state bar. The invitations were also extended to all of the members of the Pitt County Bar and members of the Pitt County judiciary.

At the ceremony each new lawyer was introduced to the court by an established member of the county bar and invited to enter the bar to take their oath as prescribed by state law. Standing at the judges' bench, I would administer the oath individually to each of the new lawyers. Upon the completion of the administration of the oaths, I gave my remarks. Each year, for the next quarter century, I read the very same remarks that I had prepared for this first ceremony.

I began, *"This day you begin your walk as a lawyer. A lawyer is a servant – servant of his community, a servant to his client and a servant to his profession. This profession that you have chosen is a walk in service to these three interests. Service to one never diminishes your obligation to the others.*

You are first a servant to your community, your state, and your country. You have just sworn to uphold the constitutions of the State of North Carolina and of the United States of America.

Maintaining a society in which the Rule of Law is observed and justice is done is your first and solemn and sworn duty of service as a lawyer. Beneath Lady Justice in the stained-glass panel behind me are the words "suum cuque tribuere" – *"To Render to Everyone His Due." This is the definition of justice. A lawyer must be an agent of order and stability, upholding the sanctity of the law, always seeking justice. You are to serve as a guardian of a strong and certain legal tradition almost a thousand years old.*

Secondly, as a lawyer you are a servant to your client. You are to see that that person's interest is protected within the parameters of the law. The representation of a client must be performed professionally and always within your obligation to uphold the rule of law and justice. Your responsibilities as a servant to your client are secondary to your obligation as a guardian of the law.

Your clients will not all be people of means who come to you with the ability to pay a handsome fee. I urge you to take the yoke of the poor upon your shoulders and provide pro bono services to the less fortunate.

Your obligation to your profession calls you to a life of integrity, honesty, and knowledge. You must do what is right thing to do in all situations and circumstances – what God, humanity, reason, and justice tell you that you ought to do.

You must be honest. Your credibility is the most valuable, yet most vulnerable asset that you possess. Without credibility among your fellow lawyers, your client, and the judges, you will have a life of trouble and frustration. This valuable possession is yours until you forfeit it with the first untruthfulness.

You must strive to be learned. There is no way for you to know all of the law – yet you must endeavor to become proficient in your calling. You must study and read the law to become the true professional. It is in this way that you become a better servant to your community and to your client.

Remember, you are a member of a family, not of lawyers—a human family. Attend to your spouse and your children. Love them and keep them, first and close.

And finally, I encourage you in the words of the late Dean Carroll Weathers of the Wake Forest Law School, "to seek justice, to walk humbly and to set the tone and character of your community." Render what is due to your community, your client, and your profession.

May God bless and keep you all.

Thankful for Justice

From the first Monday in December 1988 when I was sworn in as a District Court Judge until the 29th day of February 2016 when I retired as a Superior Court Judge, I had the wonderful privilege to serve as a judge in the courts of North Carolina. I am the most grateful person in this world for having had that opportunity. Of the twenty-seven plus years that I served as a judge, twenty-five were served in the superior court.

Behind the judge's bench in the Pitt County Courthouse are stained glass windows that I inspired and helped to design. In the middle of five panels is an exact rendering of Lady Justice as she appears on the Seal of the North Carolina Supreme Court. The motto of that great court appears below the blindfolded Lady Justice: *Suum Cique Tribuere*, "to give each his due," Justinian's definition of justice. What a beautiful thing. We are so blessed to have a place, a courthouse, where we can carry our criminal and civil burdens and find true justice. Although it is not perfect, the administration of our court system—the manner in which we provide a forum for those wronged and injured, with the ultimate fact-finder being the common man, the common jury—is the most magnificent system of justice ever imagined by man.

The court is the place, much like the city gate in ancient times, where we go to seek justice. It is a place where we attempt to give each who appears his due. The trial court is no place to attempt social engineering. That is a windmill better left to the imaginings and appetites of the legislature. At the county courthouse in the trial court, the focus is on the individual defendant and his guilt or the individual victim and his due. Some fanciful notion of collective responsibility and its siren call for correction can find no lodging here. "Social justice" does not belong at a courthouse. Lady Justice is blindfolded and cannot see race, sex or any other source of bias or prejudice. In the trial court it is justice for the accused, the victim, and the community that is paramount.

In order to ponder "social justice," our Lady Justice must first lift her blindfold and sneak a peek. Social justice requires that she must first identify the tribe to which the defendant or the purported injured or victim, belongs. The individual can no longer be the principal focus of her aim, and the matter before the court diminishes as the quest for social engineering becomes her *raison d'etre*. Justice for those individuals involved no longer reigns. Once she lifts her blindfold, unnecessary considerations such as gender and race rudely tilt the balanced scales of Lady Justice. The facts of the matter before the court now make little difference. In his indignation the judge now imagines he acquires a divine right to square the circle and make things right in his own eyes. This is the path to injustice and ruin. Social justice, as it is conceived by most, is an oxymoron. Our system of justice is not concerned with the distribution of wealth or the awarding of privileges and opportunities. Social justice does not belong in a courthouse, even a courthouse quartering appellate judges.

Emblazoned across the front of the West Portico of the United States Supreme Court building is the promise "Equal Justice Under Law." Each individual person subject to the laws of the United States appears before that court looking for justice. He expects that in his case, under the law, he will be rendered what he is due. The promise must be kept regardless of his race, creed, color, or tribe. The peace and tranquility of the community, the happiness and better friendship of its citizens, and the harmony and prosperity of all, depend on equal justice under law reliably coming forth from our courthouses. It must be. As a judge, to the best of my ability, I sought to accord equal justice under law in each case appearing before me. Needless to say, there were those who disagreed with the manner with which I administered justice. Such is life.

CALL YOUR NEXT CASE

A Turtle on a Fence Post

I have heard it said that if you come upon a turtle on top of a fence post, you can rest assured that he did not get there by himself. My wife, my father and mother, Dean Carroll Weathers, Judge John Larkins, and countless others extended their hands to encourage me to take each next step. Every election spurred me on more to serve the great people of Pitt County and North Carolina. The confidence that these people showed in me shaped my will to strive to be a good judge. But we must remember that turtle is in a perilous position.

Dr. Marion Lark was a Baptist preacher. While I attended Farmville High School, Dr. Lark was the pastor at First Baptist Church in Farmville. At the seventy-fifth anniversary service commemorating the founding of First Baptist Church of Farmville, my wife and family and I arrived late and found ourselves conspicuously seated on the very front row of the church, a very uncomfortable spot for a lifelong

Baptist. As Dr. Lark began his remarks, with a broad smile, he looked down at me and said, "And here is Rusty Duke, a judge. When he was in high school I did not know on *which* side of the law he would fall." And I can't deny that I gave him good reason to wonder.

From my earliest memory of my father, he was the man who consistently gave me the most beneficial guidance. Throughout my entire life, as a young boy and as a grown man and until his passing in 1998, if he told me once then he told me ten thousand times, "You never go wrong doing what's right." He blessed me in so many ways. He was a walking sermon before my very eyes. He encouraged me to stand firm and concentrate on being a good man in all respects. Although he was a very good businessman, he remained humble and he always seemed to be aware of life's unfortunate twists and turns. He said to me more than once that he may not leave me a large estate, but he promised that he would leave me a good name. From the time that I was a little fellow until the day he died, he always told me how proud he was of me.

My father showed me the importance of treating every individual with fairness and with the respect that person is due as a human being. I watched him closely. While campaigning for election I came upon a short man and his wife outside of the polling place in Bell Arthur, a small township in Pitt County. I introduced myself to them and asked for their vote. They looked at me and the man said to me,

"Your deddy put me to riding when nobody else would. He gave me credit and he sold me a car for a fair price when I didn't have any money. That was in the sixties, and that car ran a long time. Yes Sir, we're going to vote for you."

In the early sixties, growing up in Farmville, I would work at my father's Buick dealership. James Johnson, one of the finest men I ever knew, worked there and taught me how to wash and detail cars. He was very methodical and meticulous in the performance of every aspect of his job. He was a very good employee. Forty years later, while visiting James in his last days at his home in Falkland, he asked me, "Judge, did you know that your father helped me to get this home for me and my family?" I responded that I did not know that.

"Yes," he said, "One day I went to your dad and told him that I had a chance to get a really good job at Union Carbide in Greenville. Your dad had helped me to get this lot here and I hated to sort of walk away from him and his helping hand. It looked like that I was not grateful for what he had done for me. He had gone on my note and I was still paying on it. Your dad looked at me and said, 'James, you've got a wife and children. You need to do what's best for you and your family, and that's a very good opportunity.' I left and went to Union Carbide. When I got ready to build this house I discovered that the lot wasn't big enough to qualify for an FHA loan. Your dad went to the man who originally sold me the lot and got him to expand the lot so that it would qualify." As I sat there with my mentor it was very apparent that he was a grateful man. James then proudly showed me a magazine from UCLA with a large picture of his son on its cover, with an article recognizing his outstanding accomplishments at the university. His son later moved to Durham, where he is a prominent citizen.

My mother was a homemaker. She was my confidante, and she would always sit and listen to me. From the time I could walk she allowed me to be a boy. I would go out the door in the morning with my faithful dog, Fuzzy (named after the cowboy actor Fuzzy Q. Jones). The two of us would explore the town of Farmville, the greatest town that I have ever known. Returning after a morning out, I would join my two sisters and father for lunch at home. My mother would always have a big "dinner" prepared. Fuzzy and I would then continue our adventures with various friends for the remainder of the day. As I grew up I carried the afternoon newspaper, *The Daily Reflector*, and my mother would help me with the bookkeeping on Saturday afternoons. She provided a loving, stable home where she allowed me to keep my large bedroom floor full of toy cars and my Lionel train ready for play. In her later years, my sisters and my wife and I would take her on annual road trips to Florida, a beautiful state that she and my father had enjoyed in their early years.

I think that I have always just been myself, my own man. I have never been conscious of having any particular style or felt any yearning to be someone else. I didn't think about being like a judge, whatever that way may have been. I hope that most people would say of me, "What you see is what you get." Building a reputation of any kind was not a conscious pursuit of mine. I was intent on doing what was right within the law. I was just myself. I've always been comfortable in my own britches.

I had to work hard in school and I attained average grades. At Wake Forest Law School I had the opportunity to meet a great man, Dean Carroll Weathers. His advice echoed my father's: "You never go wrong doing what's right." Dean Weathers taught the legal ethics course, instilling in me the highest ethical standards and convincing me that being a lawyer was a high calling. He taught me that it was my duty to always be above reproach in all my conduct. Dean Weathers was a walking sermon and a great man.

United States District Court Judge John D. Larkins, Jr. was my next great mentor. After my graduation from Wake Forest Law School my wife and I moved to Trenton, a town of about four hundred souls, so that I could join Judge Larkins as a law clerk. He was an old-time North Carolina politician who had been appointed by President John F. Kennedy to sit as a federal judge in the Eastern District of North Carolina. He was a constant companion and teacher who gave me an indelible notion of how a judge ought to conduct himself and his court. Although a very friendly and gregarious man, he put up with very little nonsense in the courtroom. He too was a walking sermon, and he gave me the inspiration to later become a judge.

I hope that I have left a legacy of being an honest and dignified judge, both inside and outside the courtroom, a caretaker of the law who was fair and who patiently listened to those who appeared before me. I hope that those who came into my court found a fair judge who demanded respect for the law and the institution of the court, who put up with very little nonsense, who started the day on time, who worked hard, and who did not have time to waste. I hope that each person who entered my courtroom charged with a crime feared the law and the consequences of breaking the law. I hope that all who appeared found a judge who was impartial, who followed the law and did not attempt to mold it or expand its fearsome grasp.

It is with a sincerely grateful heart that I give to the people of Pitt County my eternal thanks for choosing me to be a trial judge in their courthouse. It is to the people in the county that I owe my appreciation and respect. It was the people who placed their trust in me to serve them as a judge. Thank you. And may the Lord bless you.

Acknowledgments

During the writing of this book I have been very fortunate to receive much encouragement and cheering on from my wife, Patsy, my children and my friends. It is impossible to repay them for their urging and boosting. Mark Martin, an accomplished trial judge, appellate judge, and law school dean, is a natural encourager. His faith, friendship and sound counsel have been a great inspiration, and I am grateful that he agreed to write my foreword.

I began to think about writing a book of my stories when it seemed that almost everyone with whom I shared a court tale responded with, "You ought to write a book!" On a trip out to California, my wife and I visited Pebble Beach Golf Club and I bought a copy of Arnold Palmer's "A Life Well Played." I loved the book of Palmer's stories. On our return from California and with encouragement from my wife, I began to write my stories of my experiences in court.

I am very fortunate to have worked with Bethany

Bradsher, who is an accomplished writer. Bethany has kept me on track by constant encouragement and meticulous editing. Stephanie Dicken designed the cover and the book, and Amanda Nichols took the photo for the cover.

My wife has spent hours editing, as have my daughter, Katherine, and my former court reporter, Allyson McNiff. To these wonderful people and those mentioned above, I say, "Thank you!" I hope that they have had as much fun as I have. There are no words that I can write here to express my deep appreciation to these friends.

CALL YOUR NEXT CASE

ASAP PHOTO & VIDEO

Members of the Pitt County Bar pose at the ceremonial grand opening of the restored Superior Courtroom #1. The judges pictured in the back row, left to right, are: Judges, back row, next to stained glass, left to right: Malcolm B Howard, Jr., John B Lewis Jr., Marvin K Blount, Jr., Wilton Russell Duke, Jr., I. Beverly Lake, Jr., Paul B. Newby, Clifton White Everett, Jr., David Leach, Thomas D. Haigwood, Gwyn Hilburn, Joseph Blick, Robert Browning, Eleanor Farr, Clerk of Superior Court, and Galen Braddy.

Made in the USA
Columbia, SC
13 January 2025

8344d831-0fbb-4cf2-a0c8-62017886b12cR01